HOW'S YOUR DRINK?

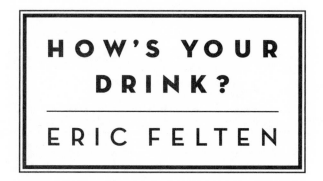

HOW'S YOUR DRINK?

ERIC FELTEN

Cocktails, Culture,

AND THE

Art of Drinking Well

Surrey Books

An **AGATE** Imprint

Chicago

Library of Congress Cataloging-in-Publication Data

Felten, Eric.

How's your drink? : cocktails, culture, and the art of drinking well / Eric Felten.

p. cm.

Summary: "A cultural history of the cocktail. Includes drink recipes"
—Provided by publisher.

ISBN-13: 978-1-57284-089-8 (hardback)

ISBN-10: 1-57284-089-7 (hardback)

1. Cocktails. 2. Cocktails—History. I. Title.

TX951.F46 2007

641.8'74—dc22

2007025700

10 9 8 7 6 5 4 3 2 1

Surrey Books is an imprint of Agate Publishing, Inc. Agate books are available
in bulk at discount prices. For more information, go to agatepublishing.com.

for Jennifer

TABLE OF CONTENTS

APERITIF

ON THE EVENING OF WEDNESDAY, APRIL 7, 1779, SAMUEL JOHNSON went to dinner at the house of Sir Joshua Reynolds; soon, according to his biographer, James Boswell, he was haranguing the guests "upon the qualities of different liquors." Offered a glass of claret, Johnson bellowed, "Poor stuff! No, Sir, claret is the liquor for boys; port, for men; but he who aspires to be a hero," he said with a smile, "must drink brandy."

Few of us look to a glass to make us heroes—Dutch courage notwithstanding—but Johnson was neither the first nor the last to recognize that what we drink speaks volumes about us. We might like to think it is a matter of no social import whether we order Manhattans or Milwaukee's Best, but we know better. Longneck bottles of brew are, to paraphrase the good doctor, the liquor for college boys; and in our time, aspiring heroes have been instructed to drink highballs.

During the glory days of the space program, the Air Force brass went to great lengths to groom hotshot pilots to be anointed astronauts.

It wasn't just their jet-jockeying skills that got honed. They were taught what mufti to wear when not in uniform, how to make casual chitchat, and even what to drink.

"It got right down to the level of cotillion etiquette," Tom Wolfe found in *The Right Stuff*. No detail was too small. To give a polished appearance, the pilots were told to wear socks that went to the knee, "so that when they sat down and crossed their legs, no bare flesh would show between the top of the socks and bottom of the pant cuffs." To make a good impression on the round of Houston cocktail parties, the Air Force officers running the pilots' "charm school" in Washington gave the fly-boys detailed instructions for how to handle themselves at the bar.

They were told, "They should drink alcohol, in keeping with the pilot code of Flying & Drinking," Wolfe writes. But alcohol of what sort? Beer or straight whiskey might seem the natural drinks for rugged fighter pilots. But beer lacked panache, and straight whiskey might have suggested an overfamiliarity with the bottle. Martinis would come across as contrived and too rarified, and no pilot could ever pull out of the spiraling career dive that would result if he were to be seen with an umbrella drink. Thus, the military specified that at Houston get-togethers, astronaut candidates would be limited to "a tall highball, either bourbon or Scotch, and only one."

Military brass weren't crazy to think that the drink in one's hand is freighted with meaning. Many novelists look to define their characters in part by what they drink; in our most glib moments, we may do the same for ourselves. If you have a creeping suspicion that others are defining you—and judging you, too—by the drink in your hand, you're not far wrong.

"There is hardly a richer single occasion for class revelation than

2

the cocktail hour," Paul Fussell wrote in his sly and malicious little book, *Class*, "since the choice of any drink, and the amount consumed, resonates with status meaning."

Some of the more opinionated commentators on drink have insisted that there are very few choices worth making in drink. Novelist and historian Bernard DeVoto was dogmatic about the limits of respectable drinking. "Martinis, slugs of whiskey, highballs, and, if you must, an Old-Fashioned. Nothing else," he declared. "You don't care to know anybody who wants anything else." You are what you drink.

The DeVoto dogma has been embraced over the years not only in society circles, but among some of the boozier polloi as well. Serious drinkers, Gerald Carson declared in his 1963 *Social History of Bourbon*, "scorned the novelties." They drank in serious saloons, such as Tom Moran's place in Chicago, where "those who had the temerity to call for a Gin Daisy were politely requested to leave quietly."

It *is* possible to be serious about drinking without being a serious drinker, especially without taking oneself too seriously. It's never been clear to me what it is about liquor that brings out the mandarins in people. Perhaps it's a nagging social insecurity that makes for diffident drinkers. We cling defensively to uninspired, socially safe glasses. We find ourselves not unlike Philip Carey in Somerset Maugham's *Of Human Bondage*, disparaging even things we enjoy out of fear that our own tastes might be suspect. Philip is staying in a house full of students in Heidelberg, and a newly arrived guest says to him, "Is the food always as bad as it was last night?"

"It's always about the same," Philip hedges (truth be told, he had always quite enjoyed the food).

"Beastly, isn't it?"

3

"Beastly." Philip falls in line with this stranger's insistent opinion because "he did not want to show himself a person of so little discrimination as to think a dinner good which another thought execrable."

Who knows how many people have been similarly bullied by opinions like those of DeVoto, who militated against any sort of variety at the bar? "There are only two cocktails," DeVoto insisted. "The bar manuals and the women's pages of the daily press, I know, print scores of messes to which they give that honorable and glorious name. They are not cocktails, they are slops."

Nonsense. Let's not be strong-armed into thinking that variety and experimentation behind the bar is any less desirable than it is in the kitchen. Even the most punctilious of gourmets are willing to bring variety into their diet; indeed, a desire to experiment and experience new tastes is part of the foodie code. The snobbiest wine snob may abjure White Zinfandel or (famously and unmeritedly) Merlot, but one who drank only Cabernet or refused to venture beyond Bordeaux would hardly be an oenophile. Yet this is exactly what happens with strong drink.

Charles Browne, a one-term Congressman and sometime mayor of Princeton, New Jersey, was one of those culinary enthusiasts who become obdurate and narrow-minded when the subject is drink. Browne grudgingly offers about a dozen cocktails in his 1939 *Gun Club Drink Book*; it's a basic slate that includes the Martini, the Manhattan, and the Old Fashioned. As for the "hundreds of other drinks called 'cocktails,'" Browne writes, "they are mostly just small mixed drinks with a base of spirits and almost anything else added." As for the catchy names pinned on drinks, they "mean nothing, but often sound like the ravings of a dipsomaniac and probably are." Browne derides the bulk of cocktails as "foolish drinks," and no doubt he had the same opinion of those who drank them.

How odd that the frothy topic of cocktails should provoke such reactionary rigidity. Spirits should, by definition, be a source of pleasure, but somehow they end up making people nervous instead. Finding a socially safe drink and sticking with it eases that anxiety. The safe choice also saves the bother of acquiring expertise in mixed drinks, and spares one the attendant disputations, worthy of philosophy graduate students, that animate the conversations of the cocktail cognoscenti—does a Sazerac take both Angostura and Peychaud's bitters, or solely the latter? It's all unnecessary if one sticks to ordering Heinekens.

But do we really want to consign ourselves to the bibulous equivalent of John Rawls' uniform? The late Harvard philosopher, author of *A Theory of Justice*, had perfected the professorial get-up: every day he wore khakis, a blue oxford button-down, and a grey herringbone sport coat. He saved himself the bother of having to choose something to wear in the morning. His routine was sensible enough—and, of course, an exercise in tedium.

Let's resolve to avoid tedium at the cocktail hour, and recognize that in some ways, drink choices are like that of wardrobe. I wouldn't wear a Hawaiian shirt to the Rainbow Room any more than I'd don a charcoal flannel suit to stroll the beach in Waikiki; by the same token, the Martini and the Mai Tai each have their time and place. To know the what, when, and where of cocktails, we need to know more than just what's tasty—the culture, the business, and even the politics of liquor. The more we know about drinks, their origins, their literature, and their lore, the better equipped we are to clothe ourselves in the right cocktails. *How's Your Drink?* is devoted to enjoying these social lubricants, and enjoying them with style.

The average bar guide runs somewhere north of a thousand recipes, and I'll agree with Charles Browne enough to admit they can't all be good. In fact, it should be no surprise that there are far more stinkers than gems. "It is only fitting that the subject of cocktails should be approached with levity slightly tinctured with contempt," wrote Lucius Beebe, a columnist for the *New York Herald Tribune* who covered the town's café society in the mid-20th century. "For every good compound, arrangement, or synthesis of liquors, wines, and their adjacent or opposite fruits and flavors chilled and served in a variety of glasses, there are approximately a million foul, terrifying, and horrendous similar excitements to stupefaction, cuspidor-hurling, and nausea." And that was written before anyone thought to combine vodka with Red Bull.

Yet, the vast, bewildering variety of possibilities—good and bad—presented by mixed drinks amounts to an adventure. There's always a discovery waiting to be made, and even the old standbys warrant endless tinkering. That was the appeal of cocktails to Crosby Gaige, whose peculiarly American life was such a fantastical combination of incongruous pursuits and interests, successes and failures as to have been a cocktail of its own.

The son of a small-town postmaster, Gaige became one of the most famous culinary connoisseurs in the country and a legendary collector of recipes and wines. He worked his way through school first by selling religious books door to door, and then by stringing for the *New York Times* and reading manuscripts for a theatrical agent. He later produced a slew of plays on Broadway, including the Pulitzer Prize-winning *Why Marry?*, and published exclusive small-run books. In 1928, Gaige published a short work by James Joyce—*Anna Livia*

Plurabelle—that Joyce later incorporated into *Finnegan's Wake*. Gaige acquired a fortune, ran an oil company, went broke, acquired a fortune's worth of debts, and then dug his way out. Somehow, he found the time to author a couple of charming books on drinks, including *Crosby Gaige's Cocktail Guide and Ladies' Companion* in 1941.

Among his varied passions, Gaige loved inventions. When the Patent Office sold off its vast collection of the models inventors were once required to submit with their patent applications, Gaige bought the bulk of them for $50,000. It was his admiration of invention that seems to have inspired his interest in cocktails. "In the world of potables, the cocktail represents adventure and experiment. All other forms of drinking are more or less static," Gaige wrote. "Beer drinkers lead a dreary and gaseous life," Gaige declared, whereas "the cocktail contriver ... has the whole world of nature at command."

Charles H. Baker, Jr., in his whimsical 1939 classic, *The Gentleman's Companion: An Exotic Drinking Book*, states the case for the cocktail in all its variety as the apogee of American inventiveness: "Whether the rest of the world cares to admit it or not," Baker brags, "we started these drinks in circulation, just as we started the telephone, submarine, phonograph, incandescent light, electric refrigerator, and decent bath tubs."

Is it daunting to take up the mantle of Edison armed only with shaker, jigger, and bottle? Maybe, but that's the fun of it. If you're lucky in your quest, some of the drinks will even taste good too. I hope you will find the drinks in this book worth the effort to make, and even if there are a few that are not to your liking, perhaps the tales of these cocktails will provide some compensatory amusement.

So let's crack some ice, limber up the shaker, and get going.

1

OF ICE AND MEN

H.L. MENCKEN WONDERED WHY "THE ETYMOLOGIES OF BOOZOLOGY" —the origins of words such as *cocktail* and *highball*—were "quite as dark as the origins of the things themselves." The sage of Baltimore suspected that "there may be something in the fact that men learned in the tongues commonly carry their liquor badly." On the other side of the coin, barroom pedants tend toward Cliff-Clavinesque flights of ersatz erudition. For his book *The American Language*, Mencken collected some 40 or 50 amateur explanations of where the term *cocktail* comes from: "Nearly all of them," he reported with sadness, "are no more than baloney."

No one knows when or where the first drink called a cocktail was mixed. We do know that a little more than 200 years ago, the first full-blown description of a "cock-tail" made it into print. According to the *Oxford English Dictionary*, the word "cocktail" first appeared in 1803 in a publication called the *Farmer's Cabinet*, but there was no explanation of what sort of drink this cocktail was—other than that it was "excellent for the head." On May 6, 1806, the word turned up again, this time in the *Balance and Columbian Repository*, a Federalist newspaper in Hudson, New York, where it figured in one of the paper's regular jibes at the party of President Thomas Jefferson.

"Rum! Rum! Rum!" read the paper's headline. "It is conjectured, that the price of this precious liquor will soon rise at Claverack," the *Balance* wrote, given that a candidate there for the state legislature must have used up the town's stocks of alcohol in a frenzy of boozy vote-buying. According to the *Balance*, the candidate had served up 720 rum-grogs, 17 dozen brandies, 32 gin-slings, 411 glasses of bitters and 25 dozen "cock-tails." Apparently, all this generosity with refreshment was for naught, the newspaper teased, as the candidate lost.

No description of those 300 cocktails there. But that week, a reader of the paper inquired as to what that mysterious concoction could possibly be, writing that he had heard of a "phlegm-cutter and fog driver, of wetting the whistle, of moistening the clay, of a fillip, a spur in the head, quenching a spark in the throat," but "never did I hear of cock tail before." On May 13, the editor of the *Balance* responded, saying that he made "it a point, never to publish anything (under my editorial head) but which I can explain." A *cock-tail* is "vulgarly called a bittered sling," he explained. That is, the drink is "a stimulating liquor, composed of spirits of any kind, sugar, water, and bitters."

The editor of the *Balance* was a man named Harry Croswell, and he had reason to be emphatic that he never published anything that he couldn't back up. He had been prosecuted just two years before on charges of "criminal libel" for publishing disparaging copy about

Jefferson—a case that provoked fundamental changes in the protection of press freedoms in America.

Harry Croswell had been happy to reprint all sorts of gossip about Jefferson, including the rumor that the President canoodled with Sally Hemings. Croswell also reported that Jefferson had given money to a man named James Callender, who had authored a notorious screed against George Washington, *The Prospect Before Us*. Callender's pamphlet had tarnished Washington and his successor, John Adams, enough to help win the election of 1800 for Jefferson. Croswell was one of several newspapermen to make a blunt accusation of dirty tricks: "Jefferson paid Callender for calling Washington a traitor, a robber, and a perjurer."

The Callender affair was starting to get uncomfortable, and Jefferson decided to go after the noisome Federalist newspapers—or rather, he quietly asked his cronies at the state level to do it for him. He wrote to his friend, the governor of Pennsylvania, that the "press ought to be restored to its credibility" and that "I have therefore long thought that a few prosecutions of the most prominent offenders would have a wholesome effect." Prosecutors in several states obliged, including New York, where Harry Croswell was charged with "deceitfully, wickedly and maliciously devising ... to detract from, scandalize, traduce, and vilify" Thomas Jefferson.

Croswell's defense was a simple one: Jefferson had indeed given the anti-Washington scribbler Callender $100. The defense team asked to bring Callender into the court to confirm as much under oath. Instead, the judge ruled that "the truth of the matter published cannot be given in evidence," and the jury found the editor guilty.

Croswell's appeal was argued by Alexander Hamilton himself. In a bravura six-hour oration that stretched over two days, Hamilton demanded to know "whether Mr. Jefferson be guilty or not of so foul an act as the one charged." The press could not be free if it could not publish the truth, he said, even if that truth cast an unflattering light "on government or individuals." Three of the four judges hearing the appeal were Jeffersonians, and the court let Croswell's conviction stand. However, swayed by Hamilton's eloquence, the New York legislature promptly passed a new law making the truth a trump in libel cases. *The People v. Croswell* remains essential reading in Press Law 101.

Two years after his trial for criminal libel, Croswell was still sticking it to the party of Jefferson. He wrote that a cock-tail "is supposed to be an excellent electioneering potion inasmuch as it renders the heart stout and bold, at the same time that it fuddles the head." And then "It is said also, to be of great use to a democratic candidate: because, a person having swallowed a glass of it, is ready to swallow any thing else."

As Croswell described them, the Gin Slings bought by the candidate in Claverack would have been a pretty simple affair—liquor, sugar, and water. Add bitters and you've got a "cock-tail." Over the years, as cocktails become ever more fanciful, the original plain sort of sling came to be seen as somewhat homely by contrast. To survive, the drink evolved, with some recipes adding lemon juice and either sweet vermouth or sherry, and some replacing the drab old water with lively seltzer. Add some bitters, and you've got a drinkable recreation of the cocktail, version 1.0. Two hundred years after the first description of a cocktail, it's no longer Hoyle to ply voters with drink. But if it were, the rather more elaborate sort of bittered gin sling would make for an excellent electioneering potion indeed.

BITTERED GIN SLING

1 ½ oz gin
¾ oz sweet vermouth or sherry
½ oz lemon juice
½ oz simple (sugar) syrup
A dash or two of Angostura bitters
Soda water

Shake all but the fizzy water with ice. Strain into a tumbler or high-ball glass over ice, and top with soda. Garnish with lemon peel.

Cocktails were hardly the first mixed drinks in the world; among the ancient Greeks, no self-respecting symposiarch would think of serving wine that hadn't first been cut with water. The word *julep* has its origin in Persia—just as the word *alcohol* itself can be traced back over the centuries to Arabic. Colonial America was awash in concoctions called *smashes* and *shrubs*. But though the word *cocktail* turned up first in the *Farmer's Cabinet* and was first described in the *Balance*, we still don't know where the word came from.

Not that there's any shortage of would-be etymologies. In his 1821 novel *The Spy*, James Fenimore Cooper credited a Westchester, New York, barmaid with creating the first *cock-tail*. Elizabeth "Betty" Flanagan was saucy—literally and figuratively: "Her faults were, a trifling love of liquor, excessive filthiness, and a total disregard to all the decencies of language." Cooper wrote that it was no accident Betty came up with so worthy a new drink: "Elizabeth Flanagan was peculiarly well qualified by education and circumstances to perfect this improvement in liquors, having been brought up on its principal ingredient." Cooper was embellishing what was already a common tale of the cocktail, that a patriotic barmaid during the Revolution plucked the feathers from some local Tory's roosters (just as she might have plucked King George's beard, if he had one) and then taunted the loyalist by decorating her inn's drinks with the cocks' tails that she had stolen. A good story, but as William Grimes concluded in his book *Straight Up or On the Rocks: A Cultural History of American Drink*, a "thoroughly spurious anecdote." As Grimes puts it, "Like a bad alibi, it is at once too vague and too specific."

Among the long line of apocryphal stories attempting to answer the question (there once was a thirsty Aztec king whose daughter was named Xochitl ...), one of the most repeated and least ridiculous is the founding myth centered in New Orleans, a town still legendary for its drinking. At first glance, New Orleans might not look like much of a place for proper cocktails. Every third doorway in the French Quarter is a "Daiquiri bar"—each one the same phalanx of Slurpee-like machines behind a counter, and each awash with the same rainbow selection of swirling rum slush. Pick your favorite color of the stuff and the Daiquiri jerk pulls a lever, filling a deep plastic cup for you to take out on the street. I just happened to be in New Orleans a few weeks before Hurricane Katrina, and I didn't notice a single Daiquiri bar promising a better tasting slush than their competitors; several did, however, advertise "The World's Strongest Drink," which is some indication of the priorities at work.

But for all the industrialized bacchanal, New Orleans has traditionally been home to a remarkably civilized cocktail culture—if you find your way to the right bars. On a hot afternoon, Napoleon House is the place for a Pimm's Cup; the house cocktail at Lafitte's Blacksmith Shop is a Martini laced with faux-absinthe called an

Obituary Cocktail; up until Katrina, the Fairmont (née Roosevelt) Hotel was still shaking up the Ramos Gin Fizzes that were Huey Long's favorite. (The Kingfish was so devoted to the Ramos Gin Fizz that when he became Senator Long, he brought a man from the Roosevelt to Washington to teach a small army of D.C. bartenders how to make the drink.)

Then there's the Hotel Monteleone's Carousel Bar, where the circular bar revolves slowly under a whimsical carnival canopy of carved wood, mirrors, and bare bulbs. The barstools don't go up and down, thankfully, but the experience can still be a little disorienting; get caught up in a conversation, and the next thing you know, you're on the other side of the room. Ask bartender Marvin Allen to mix you up a Vieux Carré, a terrific drink invented by the Carousel's barman in the 1930s, and unknown to most mixologists outside of the Hotel Monteleone.

VIEUX CARRÉ

Dash Peychaud's Bitters
Dash Angostura Bitters
½ teaspoon Benedictine
1½ oz cognac
½ oz rye whiskey
½ oz sweet vermouth

Mix over ice in a short glass. Garnish with a twist of lemon.

It's fitting that New Orleans should have a thriving cocktail culture, given that the cocktail, not jazz, has long been claimed to be the first American art form born in the Crescent City. The story goes that sometime around the turn of the 19th century, a Creole apothecary named Antoine Peychaud started mixing his medicinal bitters with sugar and cognac and serving them up at his pharmacy in a French eggcup called a *coquetier*. English-speakers soon corrupted the word to *cocktail*. The story is spurious, to be sure; the timeline is such that old Antoine couldn't have even bittered his first brandy when *cocktail* turned up in print way up north in Yankee territory.

But it's still as good a story as any, mainly because it provides a plausible reason for the drink's particular ingredients: liquor, sugar, and bitters. Edward Henry Durell, writing under the pseudonym "H. Didimus," describes being introduced to the "brandy cocktail" in New Orleans around 1840, and he makes it clear that it's the bitters that made the drink. As late as 1934, *Webster's* still defined a cocktail as "a short drink, iced, of spirituous liquor well mixed with flavoring ingredients, commonly including bitters."

Why bitters? Back before the Pure Food and Drug Act of 1906 put the kibosh on snake oil, bitters—herb-and-root tinctures—were a thriving category in the patent medicine business. Visit the 19th-century New Orleans pharmacy on Chartres Street that's now a museum and you'll find shelves full of old bottles of Boker's Bitters, Stoughton's Bitters, Hofstetter's Stomach Bitters, and Gold Lion Celery Bitters (not far from Brodie's Diarrhea Cordial). By the looks of the stuff, a spoonful of sugar just might not have been enough to make the medicine go down, and that's where the brandy comes in. The surprise wasn't that the medicine was more palatable with a slug of liquor, but that the liquor benefited from the complex herbal flavors in the bitters.

Cocktails have long since come to mean just about any mixed drink. That, and certain advances in medicine over the last hundred years, have wreaked havoc with the bitters biz. Angostura persists, but Peychaud's—with its spicy, peppery quality suggestive of cinnamon Altoids—would probably have gone the way of Hofstetter's and Boker's and the rest if it weren't for New Orleans' private social clubs. The members of the Pickwick Club, among others, continued over the decades to drink obscure, traditional New Orleans cocktails that call for Peychaud's bitters in quantities sufficient to keep the brand alive. That's a good thing, because without Peychaud's, you can't make that most iconic of New Orleans cocktails, the Sazerac, which traces its lineage all the way back to Antoine Peychaud's apothecary shop.

I tried a slew of Sazeracs in the Crescent City, and the best by far was the one crafted for me by the dean of New Orleans bartenders, Chris McMillian. He holds court evenings at the Library Lounge in the Ritz-Carlton, where he mixes superb cocktails and shares what he's learned researching the history of American drinks.

The Sazerac takes its name from a brand of cognac popular in New Orleans in the 19th century, but by the 1890s, the cognac was out and rye whiskey was in. McMillian puts two heavy-bottomed, short glasses on the bar. One he fills with ice to chill; in the other, he mixes the drink. He tosses a dash each of Peychaud's and Angostura bitters onto a sugar cube, together with a small splash of water. He crushes the sugar with a muddler (the bar equivalent of a pestle) until it is thoroughly dissolved.

McMillian adds Old Overholt Rye to the bitters-and-sugar mixture and stirs it with ice. Out of the other glass he tosses the ice and into it he puts a tablespoon's worth of Herbsaint, a substitute for the now-illegal Absinthe that would have been used in Peychaud's day. He spins that glass in the air to give the inside an even coating of the green liqueur and then lets the excess drip out. Into that glass, McMillian strains the ice-cold rye that's been stained red by the bitters, and then he gives it a lemon twist.

It may not be the World's Strongest Drink, but the Sazerac, with its spicy-sweet contradictions, is a cocktail according to the original specifications. Taste one, and you'll realize why the concept caught on.

SAZERAC

1 cube of sugar
2 dashes Peychaud's Bitters
2 oz rye whiskey or cognac
Herbsaint or Ricard liqueur

Dissolve sugar in bitters and a splash of water. Stir with whiskey or cognac and ice. Strain into an Herbsaint-coated glass. Lemon twist.

Even after the cocktail began its inexorable march of conquest over the world of drink, there was no shortage of conservative souls who militated for the old standbys that the cocktail had begun to displace, especially in stodgy old England. By the late 1800s, venerable colonial favorites like the Shrub were scarce in the States but still going strong in Britain. As late as the mid-19th century, the British parliament was still grappling with how to regulate the booming trade in "rum-shrub" coming from the U.S.

"There never was any liquor so good as rum shrub." That rather bold endorsement comes by way of William Makepeace Thackeray, in a serialized novel with the wonderful title, *The Adventures of Philip on His Way Through the World: Showing Who Robbed Him, Who Helped Him, and Who Passed Him By*. Shrub turns up time and again in Thackeray's stories, perhaps most famously when a bottle of Shrub is responsible for turning schoolboy William Dobbin into the hero of *Vanity Fair* (well, at least as much of a hero as one can get in a book subtitled *A Novel Without a Hero*).

A school bully named Cuff has sent scrawny little George Osbourne "to run a quarter of a mile; to purchase a pint of rum-shrub on credit" and to sneak the bottle back to the school playground. The poor little fellow slips coming over the wall, and the bottle is shattered. "How dare you, sir, break it?" bellows the bully. "You blundering little thief. You drank the shrub, and now you pretend to have broken the bottle. Hold out your hand, sir." Cuff proceeds to thwack the trembling, moaning child's hand with a cricket stump again and again—until Dobbin steps in. He promises to give Cuff "the worst thrashing you ever had in your life." Which is exactly what he does.

Shrub has likely not been implicated in any brawls for more than a century, so completely has it fallen out of use. But once upon a time, it was as popular as it was versatile. Shrub per se refers to a style of fruit syrup born in colonial America. Usually made with vinegar, the syrup could sit on the shelf for long, unrefrigerated stretches. The syrup could be mixed with cold water for a refreshing summer soft drink, or—more often than not in the well-lubricated days of the Founding Fathers—rum or some other spirit rounded out the glass. One of the few places you can find the drink on the menu today is Philadelphia's City Tavern, which combines waiters in breeches and mob-capped waitresses with serious colonial-style cuisine. At the City Tavern, you can get your Shrub mixed with rum, brandy, or Champagne. However you take it, a few sips will show why Shrub had such a long run.

The shrub boom may be long passed, but the drink can easily be recreated if you have a shrub syrup to start with. Boil a cup of water and dissolve a cup of sugar in it. Drop the heat, add two pints of raspberries, and let it all simmer for 10 minutes. Next, add two cups of white wine vinegar, and bring the pot up to a boil for a couple of minutes. Strain it, cool it, and bottle it: refrigerated, the Shrub should keep for months.

RASPBERRY RUM SHRUB

1 oz raspberry shrub syrup
2 oz dark rum
4 oz ginger ale or soda water

Build with ice in a stemmed goblet, and stir.
Garnish with fresh raspberries.

RASPBERRY SHRUB SYRUP

1 cup sugar
1 cup water
2 pints raspberries
2 cups white wine vinegar

Whisk water and sugar together at a boil. Reduce heat for a few minutes and add raspberries, stirring occasionally, for 10 min. Add vinegar and bring to a boil for 2 min. Strain, cool, and bottle. Keep refrigerated (even if the Founding Shrubbers didn't).

[RECIPE COURTESY OF WALTER STAIB, CHEF OF PHILADELPHIA'S CITY TAVERN.]

But why bother, when Pennsylvania's Tait Farm makes luscious shrub syrups in a variety of flavors using their own fresh fruit vinegars. Tait Farm sells raspberry, cherry, strawberry, cranberry, and ginger shrub syrups in bottles large or small at its website, www.tait-farmfoods.com. Though raspberry is my favorite of the bunch, they are all delicious.

The notion of putting any sort of vinegar in a drink may be counterintuitive—or even off-putting. Remember, however, that mixed drinks generally strive for a balance between sweet and tart. In most cocktails, the tart comes from limes, lemons, or other citrus; the vinegar in the shrub syrup serves the same purpose.

The Shrub found itself shoved aside to make room for newfangled cocktail contraptions, but another iconic American drink that predates the cocktail, the Julep, managed to survive (even if the drink has become as rare as sightings of black panthers in Florida). Part of the enduring appeal of the Julep has been its leisurely pace. Cocktails in the truest sense are compact concoctions sized to be finished off in a few gulps. The Julep, by contrast, delivers a large load of liquor but suspends it in finely crushed and densely packed ice, from which it can be accessed only with a civilized languor. Woe to the drinker who, failing to recognize the difference between a Julep and a cocktail, tries to drink the former like the latter.

Juleps "are drunk so seldom that when, say, on Derby Day somebody gives a julep party, people drink them like cocktails, forgetting that a good julep holds at least five ounces of Bourbon," novelist Walker Percy noted. "Men fall face-down unconscious, women wander in the woods disconsolate and amnesiac, full of thoughts of Kahlil Gibran and the limberlost." But those who appreciate juleps know to take them at a leisurely pace that contrasts with the drinking of cocktails. Teddy Roosevelt swore by the difference—literally.

You see, Harry Croswell and the Bittered Gin Sling may have been the first time that a mixed drink crossed paths with a president and a case of criminal libel, but it wasn't the last. Late one afternoon in May 1913, Theodore Roosevelt motored to Grand Central Terminal, where he boarded the Lakeshore Limited bound for the Midwest. He was joined by enough friends, relatives, and newspapermen to pack a Pullman car. Their ultimate destination was the county courthouse in Marquette, Michigan, where the former president would take the stand to prove he was no drunk.

Over the years, many mistook Colonel Roosevelt's high spirits for being under the influence of spirits. When T.R. ran for president on the "Bull Moose" ticket in 1912, the Roosevelt-haters insinuated that his bully bonhomie was nothing other than habitual drunkenness. "If this slander is ever printed in so many words," Roosevelt warned during the campaign, "I will bring suit for damages and settle it once and for all."

George Newett, editor and publisher of *Iron Ore*, the newspaper of record in Ishpeming, Michigan, soon obliged. "Roosevelt lies and curses in a most disgusting way," Newett wrote. "He gets drunk, too, and that not infrequently, and all his intimates know about it." T.R. promptly charged Newett with libel, suing him for $10,000 in damages.

When the case went to trial months later, Roosevelt's lengthy witness list included a former secretary of state, secretary of the Navy, secretary of the interior, a young cousin, one of his butlers, reporters, and various old comrades in arms. Nonetheless, the big show came when Roosevelt himself stepped into the witness box and took the oath.

"I have never been drunk or in the slightest degree under the influence of liquor," he declared at the start of his nearly two hours of testimony. "I never drank a cocktail or a highball in my life." Instead, Roosevelt allowed that he might have one glass of "light wine" with dinner, a glass of Champagne when protocol demanded it, and perhaps a "measured spoonful of brandy" in a glass of milk before bed when the doctor prescribed it. Oh, and yes, Mint Juleps.

"There was a fine bed of mint at the White House," the old Rough Rider remembered. "I may have drunk half a dozen Mint Juleps in a year." Roosevelt's lawyer got a good guffaw from the courtroom when he asked, "Did you drink them all at one time?"

For all the laughter, the trial was no joke. With Prohibition less than a decade away, the forces for and against alcohol were at each other's wet and dry throats. The temperance crusade had long targeted prominent politicians, with some success. Back in the 1870s, First Lady "Lemonade" Lucy Hayes convinced her husband Rutherford to ban booze from the White House. As Roosevelt biographer Kathleen Dalton puts it, "Drinking was the abortion issue of T.R.'s day." A politician had to decide whether to be pro-highlife or anti-libation. By portraying himself as a man who enjoyed drinks in abstemious moderation, T.R. managed a straddle of Clintonian sophistication: He may have sipped the occasional Mint Julep, but he didn't inhale them.

Roosevelt testified that in the years since he left the White House he had put only two Mint Juleps to his lips. One of those, he said, was at the St. Louis Country Club, where he only took a couple of sips. The *St. Louis Post Dispatch* teasingly accused T.R. of perjury. After all, the Mint Juleps made by the country club's bartender, Tom Bullock, were just too good for anyone to taste and put aside. "To believe that a red-blooded man, and a true Colonel at that, ever stopped with just a part of one of those refreshments," the *Post Dispatch* editorialized, "is to strain credulity too far."

But perhaps, just perhaps, the Julep T.R. sampled at the St. Louis

Country Club simply disappointed. Tom Bullock penned a bar book titled *The Ideal Bartender* (the preface to which was written by a club member, one George Herbert Walker, grandfather and great-grandfather to presidents himself). Though his recipe for "Mint Julep, Kentucky style" was correct, it was a rather basic affair—sugar, mint, ice and bourbon—and hardly the fruity, elaborate concoction Roosevelt had come to savor in his White House days.

During the Colonel's administration, from 1901 to 1909, White House steward Henry Pinckney was in charge of the Juleps. When he sensed that T.R. had built up a thirst, he was off to the mint patch, which, according to a *Washington Post* account from 1913, was on the White House grounds "back of the executive offices, behind a lattice-work house, where they hang the clothes to dry."

Pinckney would start in best Julep fashion by putting a few mint leaves in the bottom of a glass with a lump of sugar and a splash of water. "With a silver crusher, he would bruise the leaves with the greatest care." Once the sugar was dissolved into a nice minty syrup, he would add not the bourbon found in a Kentucky-style Julep, but instead a few drops of brandy and a "good 'slug' of rye whiskey of the finest kind procurable."

Then, Pinckney filled the glass to its rim with cracked ice, but the true measure of his artistry was just beginning. As is traditional, into the top of the drink Pinckney would stick "a sprig of mint, so that the leaves dangled about temptingly." And then, piled high on the ice, Pinckney arrayed "a bountiful supply of cherries, sliced pineapple, banana, and orange." Carmen Miranda had nothing on the Colonel's Juleps.

Back at the Marquette County Courthouse, Newett's defense team had found only one witness prepared to say he had seen Roosevelt drunk—and he had to lam it to Canada to escape a bad-check rap. Newett knew when he was licked. The editor stood and read a statement in court: "I am forced to the conclusion that I was mistaken." Magnanimously, Roosevelt waived his demand for damages, and the court awarded him a token judgment of exactly six cents.

The *Washington Post*, in one of the great headlines of the century, described the aftermath: "COLONEL QUAFFS MILK: Celebrates Libel Suit Victory With Bovine Bumpers." Bully!

T.R.'S LIBELOUS MINT JULEP

4 oz rye whiskey
¼ oz brandy
Fresh mint
1 sugar cube
Sliced pineapple, sliced banana, orange slices and cherries

*Gently muddle a few leaves of mint with the sugar and
a good splash of water in the bottom of a glass (or silver Julep cup,
if you have one). Add brandy and whiskey, and then fill the cup
to the rim with pulverized ice. Stir until the outside of the glass is thick
with frost. Pile the top of the drink high with mint and fruit.*

It is only fitting that an American icon like Teddy Roosevelt drank Juleps, which are perhaps the iciest of iced drinks. It's not just that ice—whether cubed, crushed, cracked, shaved, frappéd, pulverized or puréed—makes the drink. It's that ice is itself the defining characteristic of American drinks.

It's no accident. The gospel of ice-cold beverages was spread the world over by a Boston merchant, who in 1805 had the brilliant, crazy idea that the sweaty souls of sun-wracked ports in the West Indies would pay anything to get their hands on ice from the ponds that froze every year in the Massachusetts winter. Though he was met at first with ridicule, Frederic Tudor was convinced the scheme would make him "inevitably and unavoidably rich," and stuck to it with a determination that bordered on obsession. After decades of setbacks and near ruin—Tudor was in and out of debtor's prison, and regularly had to hide from the local sheriff—the business of sailing ice from Boston to the steamier latitudes did indeed make Frederic Tudor a wealthy man. His ice ships made regular deliveries to ports as close as Charleston and New Orleans, and as far away as Calcutta.

The venture was hardly the no-brainer that Tudor at first imagined it would be. Gavin Weightman's history of *The Frozen Water Trade* recounts that on his first voyage, Tudor's ship lost its masts in a storm. They were other hazards and hurdles: Pirates still prowled the Caribbean; tropical islands were known for the palms...of the local officials looking for bribes; and, rather inconveniently, Tudor kept losing his sales agents to yellow fever. Nonetheless, it turned out that Tudor was right about the technical feasibility of his scheme—properly insulated with a thick layer of sawdust, a shipload of ice could sail for months in tropical waters with a minimum of melting.

At first, Tudor's biggest problem was that few in the tropics knew what to do with the ice he had brought from so far away. He soon figured out how to manufacture demand: cocktails.

The Ice King's marketing plan, laid out to his sales agent in Martinique, involved a loss leader: Give free ice to all the local cafes. "A man who has drank his drinks cold at the same expense for one week," Tudor wrote, "can never be presented with them warm again."

What sort of drinks did Tudor promote? He pushed concoctions that weren't just cold, but deliciously slushy with ice, such as the Smash. As Harry Craddock would put it in his 1930 *Savoy Cocktail Book*, a Smash "is in effect a Julep on a small plan." Like a Julep, it is made by muddling sugar and mint in the bottom of a glass—in the case of a Smash, however, it would be a short glass. Fill with shaved ice, pour in just about any sort of liquor, and stir.

BRANDY SMASH

1 tsp sugar
3 or 4 mint leaves
1 ½ oz brandy
¼ oz Benedictine

In a short glass, gently crush the mint in the sugar with a splash of water. Fill the glass with well-crushed ice, add the brandy and Benedictine, and stir. Garnish with a sprig of mint, and if you like, cut a straw in half and stick the two halves in the glass.

Tudor knew that to make ice a necessity born of habitual use, it had to be always available, and that meant going to extraordinary lengths to keep his tropical ice-houses stocked with frozen water. When, early in the enterprise, Boston experienced a winter warm enough to give Al Gore the vapors, there wasn't enough pond ice for Tudor to harvest. Undaunted, he hired a ship to sail north to the Arctic ice floes, where the crew grappled and boarded an iceberg, chopped it up, and filled the ship's hold.

Tudor's most audacious gamble came in 1833, when he outfitted a ship to carry ice to India. Not only did the cargo arrive intact, it caused a sensation. "The names of those who planned and have successfully carried through the adventure at their own cost," the *Calcutta Courier* raved, "deserve to be handed down to posterity with the names of other benefactors of mankind."

This isn't to say that everyone was happy with the enterprise. Back on the other side of the world, Henry David Thoreau watched disapprovingly as Tudor's men noisily chopped up the ice on Walden Pond; but he did marvel that "the pure Walden water is mingled with the sacred water of the Ganges."

The *India Gazette* cheered Tudor for making "this luxury accessible, by its abundance and cheapness." Frederic Tudor took what had been considered a great luxury and turned it into a quotidian necessity. In his book on America, Alistair Cooke singled Tudor out as "the brilliant forerunner of the American businessman and advertiser at their most characteristic," letting the masses "buy at a discount the services formerly reserved for the rich."

Today—thanks at first to fierce competition in the booming ice biz, and later to electricity and the freezer—the amazing stuff is so commonplace and cheap that it has come to be seen as something of a filler, if not a nuisance. One thing Frank Sinatra would not tolerate was "not enough ice in the drink!" How much was enough? Sinatra's default drink was Jack Daniel's and water on the rocks in a none-too-large Old-Fashioned glass. According to *The Way You Wear Your Hat: Frank Sinatra and the Lost Art of Livin'* by Bill Zehme, the singer wanted his whiskey cooled by exactly four cubes. But even ice-loving Frank Sinatra would complain if the quantity of cubes started to crowd out the Jack Daniel's. "With all this ice," Sinatra once cracked to a cowering bartender, "I figure we're supposed to go skating here or something. That's not my sport."

When ice was a luxurious novelty, its quality seemed to matter. The ice that Tudor and others harvested from Wenham Lake in Massachusetts came to be so famous for its crystalline purity that it was the only thing an English society hostess would think of using. "Everyone has the same everything in London," Thackeray wrote mockingly in 1856, "You see the same coats, the same dinners, the same boiled fowls and mutton, the same cutlets, fish and cucumbers, the same lumps of Wenham Lake ice."

But now, we take ice's quality for granted, and our drinks suffer for it. We almost always chill our drinks at home with ice cranked out by the restless little machine in the freezer. By and large, these are neither cubes nor lumps, but ugly, stubby crescents. That just won't do. Happily, one can still buy ice trays—in particular, chic silicon trays made by a company called Tovolo that produce big, beautiful, square-sided cubes. What a rich, satisfying sound they make rattling in a glass, and how perfectly they chill the drink. Yes, making your cubes in trays takes a little effort, but then again, so did sailing ice from Boston to Calcutta.

At first, it was bitters that defined a drink as a cocktail. Now bitters are an afterthought, at best. But rare is the mixed drink that foregoes frozen water. Once upon a time, Brits were willing to fend off the cold with a tot of hot gin. Mr. Bumble, the small-minded Beedle of *Oliver Twist*, took his gin with hot water. Ugh. For Americans, ice is the thing. Without ice, there would be no highball; without ice, there would be no frozen Margarita. Ice is no less essential to those drinks in which it doesn't even appear, the straight-up cocktails. Without ice, after all, there would be no Martinis.

2

SLAM, BANG, TANG

MARTINI PASSIONS RUN HIGH. CONSIDER THE COPY I FOUND OF A 1930 cocktail book called *Shake 'Em Up*. In an elegant but excited hand, the first owner of the volume penciled a simple editorial comment over the book's Martini recipe: "NO, NO, NO!!!"

The *Shake 'Em Up* Martini recipe – two parts gin to one part French vermouth and a couple of dashes of bitters—was a bit archaic even in 1930. In the twelfth year of the Volstead Act, a Martini would still generally have been made with a few drops of orange bitters, but the fashionable ratio of gin to vermouth was already four to one. In decades to come, that ratio would be doubled, and then doubled again.

The Martini started life in the 1880s as the Martinez cocktail. The drink was derived from the Manhattan—whiskey, sweet vermouth, and bitters—by substituting gin for the whiskey. The gin in question was originally a syrupy-sweet (and now obscure) variety called Old Tom gin. But sweetened gin mixed with sweet vermouth still wasn't quite sugary enough for that carious-stumped age—most Martinez recipes called for a few dashes of "gum syrup" (that is, sugar water) to get it just right. By the aught years, Old Tom was tossed in favor of dry gin, the sweet (red) vermouth gave way to dry (white) vermouth, and the Martinez came to be the dry Martini.

A Martini made with dry gin and dry vermouth proved to be a far more sophisticated cocktail than its sweet predecessor. "The ultimate class bifurcation based on drink," Paul Fussell wrote, is "the difference between dry and sweet." But somewhere along the way, "dry" stopped meaning the opposite of "sweet" and came to mean the relative absence of vermouth. Even so, the social cachet attached to "dryness" persisted, and decades of striving have produced today's dry Martini standard: in effect, a straight shot of gin or vodka. Which is odd, because there's nothing particular swanky about a glass of plain gin – in George Orwell's *Nineteen Eighty-Four*, everyone gulps his synthetic gin straight.

Ladder-climbing hasn't been the only imperative driving Martini desiccation. Ernest Hemingway ranked "dry" Martini-drinking somewhere between bull fighting and big-game hunting in his hierarchy of the manly arts. Papa favored his Martini ratio at 15 to 1, and called them "Montgomerys" to mock Old Monty, the WWII British commander who, Hemingway sneered, wouldn't attack the Germans unless he had a 15 to 1 advantage in the field.

M.F.K. Fisher didn't call her cocktails Montgomerys, but her ratio was not unlike Hemingway's—she used an eyedropper to dispense the vermouth. "It seems improbable that my hint of herby wine, the tonic quality of a drop of vermouth, could possibly turn straight dry gin into a quick-working *apéritif*," she wrote in the *Atlantic Monthly* in January

1949, "but it does: chilled gin has nothing in common with this ridiculously delicious cocktail."

I wonder. Vermouth avoidance may connote social status or tough-guy panache, but it doesn't make much sense as far as the taste of the drink is concerned. Plenty of cocktails call for a dash of this or a drop of that, and in those recipes, the this-and-that are almost always intensely flavored ingredients, such as pastis or bitters. It's not unlike using vanilla extract in baking—a few drops go a long way. But vermouth is not only mild; it takes what flavor it has from some of the same botanicals that contribute to the taste of gin, including coriander, orange peel, and orris root.

Bernard DeVoto may have been a bit monomaniacal when it came to Martinis—declaring it to be just about the only mixed drink worthy of the honorific "cocktail"—but he clearly knew something about the drink and its proper construction. In his book *The Hour*, DeVoto disdains the overly dry sort of Martini. He identified the "point where the marriage of gin and vermouth is consummated" at 3.7 to 1. Much less vermouth than that and you will miss "art's sunburst of imagined delight becoming real." A ratio of 4 to 1 was also acceptable, and even "a little more than that, which is a comfort if you cannot do fractions in your head." But start messing around with 15-to-1 Martinis, DeVoto warned, and you will have obliterated the delicate charm of "the violet hour, the hour of hush and wonder, when the affections glow again and valor is reborn."

As DeVoto's prose suggests, he considered the correct composition of the Martini to be one of the great spiritual questions of the day. Great spiritual questions are always fiercely contested, particularly when no one can agree on just how much vermouth goes into the

Martinis being drunk by angels dancing on the head of a pin. Charges of apostasy fly. In the 1961 edition of his *Fine Art of Mixing Drinks*, David Embury derides DeVoto's idealized Martini: "I have found many of his comments on drinks and drink mixing thoroughly sound," Embury wrote. "But, when it comes to the Martini, phooey!" Embury objected not only to DeVoto's preferred ratio of gin to vermouth, but also to the very notion that there was only one correct specification for the cocktail. "I suppose that his absolutely perfect ratio would be something like 3.690412 to 1!"

THE BERNARD DEVOTO MARTINI

1.845206 oz gin
½ oz dry vermouth

*Fill a pitcher with "five hundred pounds of ice."
Add gin and vermouth and stir. "You must be unhurried but you
must work fast, for a diluted Martini would be a contradiction
in terms." Pour into chilled Martini glasses. Twist a lemon
peel over the top of the glass and then discard the piece of rind.*

Embury preferred an Aristotelian mean between extremes, a ratio of 7:1. (However, it's important to note in this case that the extreme opposite of the Montgomery is the *Shake 'Em Up* 2:1, not DeVoto's rather mainstream, if punctilious, 3.7:1.) Embury's recipe is a pretty good reference point for Martini-making, and it also serves as a timely reminder that extremes in drink are to be avoided.

One of the worst extremes afflicting modern Martinis is size. The three-Martini lunch isn't quite the debilitating excess that it sounds like if you realize that the Martinis of the Lunch's 1950s heyday were half, or a third, as big as today's stemmed tubs of gin. The next time you catch a bit of *North By Northwest* on television, look for the scene in which Cary Grant and Eva Marie Saint trade sexy banter in the Pullman dining car. Grant starts his meal by ordering a Gibson (a Martini garnished with a cocktail onion). The drink arrives in a glass so small that bowl and stem both disappear in his hand. It was almost certainly a better drink than today's gigantic Martinis, which are guaranteed to be warm as dishwater (and about as savory) halfway through.

The durable American fetish for gargantuan portions has been deleterious enough for food, but when it comes to drink the results have been positively disastrous. In the late '90s, the Denver branch of The Palm steakhouse chain was serving up what its bartender proudly claimed was the ultimate Martini—an 11-ounce glass of straight vodka. Putting aside the point that such a drink is no Martini, who knows how many poor souls felt compelled to guzzle their way to the bottom of that enormity, and woozily swore off any further congress with cocktails? This is hazing, not hospitality.

For all the ritual and mythology, a Martini is a perfectly easy drink to make. Start with good gin and good vermouth and the drink nearly makes itself. Happily, that's not at all hard to do. Liquor store shelves are crowded with an embarrassment of excellent gins these days. You can think of gin as basically a flavored vodka. The smell and taste of juniper berries is almost always front and center, but since a decent gin is infused with a dozen or more spices and botanicals—often including fennel, licorice, angelica root, and cassia bark—distillers have plenty of room to define their gin by the choice of which flavors to emphasize. Just be sure that the gin does indeed have flavor—some recently invented gin brands attempt to woo the vodka drinker by passing off as gin a spirit so faintly flavored as to be nearly indistinguishable from vodka.

There's no such thing as the perfect Martini, so, as the bartender in a *New Yorker* cartoon once said, a near-perfect Martini will have to do. Eyedrops of vermouth aren't enough, so the recipe falls into the range Embury suggested—seven to one—recognizing that one can use a little more or a little less, to taste.

NEAR-PERFECT MARTINI

2 oz gin
¼ - ⅓ oz dry vermouth

*Shake and/or stir with ice, and strain into a Martini glass.
Garnish with olive.*

If you have a retro sensibility and strive to enjoy the classic in its classic 1930s proportions—four parts gin to one part vermouth—be true to the era by adding a couple of dashes of orange bitters as well. It's what I call the "Original Intent Martini."

ORIGINAL INTENT MARTINI

2 oz gin
½ oz dry vermouth
2 dashes orange bitters

*Shake and/or stir with ice and strain into a Martini glass.
Garnish with olive.*

Shake your Martinis and they'll come out with a nice icy bite; stir them if you want a silkier consistency. Either way, use ice untainted by municipal chlorine and free from memories of trout caught last summer. All that's left is to decide whether to garnish your drink with an olive or a twist of lemon. The purest of the purists are militant about the slice of lemon peel, twisted ever so gently over the glass, that imparts a delicate mist of citrus oil to the Martini's surface. I prefer an olive or three (two being both bad luck and bad form) in my drink. I like the savory hint of brine that comes with the garnish in the glass, and I like eating the olives as a coda to the cocktail—who can snack on lemon peel?

These days, a Martini actually made with gin can seem quaint, a development one can blame in part on the James Bond film franchise and its insistence that Martinis be made with vodka. It isn't long into *Dr. No*—the first of the James Bond books made into a movie—that Sean Connery is served "One medium dry vodka martini, mixed like you said, sir, and not stirred." That drink formula would soon become an iconic part of the Bond mystique. Later, through sheer repetition, Bond's vodka martini became a tired punchline, as dull and formulaic as the post-Connery Bond pictures themselves. But the secret agent found in Ian Fleming's books isn't quite the slave of habit that the movie producers (with their lucrative product-placement deals) made him out to be.

James Bond's first drink on record occurs some 30 pages into Fleming's debut novel, *Casino Royale*. He strolls into a bar at a French resort hotel—a bar full of fashionable young lovelies drinking dry gin Martinis, no less—and he orders … an Americano.

A what? An Americano is made of Campari, sweet vermouth, and soda water over ice in a highball glass. One of my favorite drinks, with its perfect balance of bitter and sweet, the Americano is admittedly an acquired taste (or, in the case of my wife, a taste she has chosen not to acquire). The drink was so popular among Americans visiting Italy at the turn of the last century that it was named after them. The Americano was once even bottled as a pre-made cocktail. Nowadays, it is obscure enough to be a fair test of your favorite bartender's skills.

Bond's taste for Americano highballs is explained in the short story "From a View to a Kill," which starts with Bond licensed to kill time in Paris. "One cannot drink seriously in French cafes," Fleming writes. "Out of doors on a pavement in the sun is no place for vodka or whisky or gin." Instead, one makes the best of the "musical comedy drinks" appropriate to the venue, in which case "Bond always had the same thing—an Americano."

AMERICANO HIGHBALL

1½ oz Campari
1½ oz sweet vermouth
Soda water

Pour Campari and vermouth over ice in a highball glass.
Top with soda water. Garnish with orange peel.

Ian Fleming knew that in drink, no less than in food, it pays to play to an establishment's strength. When Bond grabs a roadhouse lunch with Felix Leiter in *Diamonds Are Forever*, he doesn't waste time elucidating the comparative virtues of shaking versus stirring; he just orders a beer (a Miller High Life, at that).

When in Jamaica, 007 favors Gin and Tonics extra heavy on juice from the island's fresh limes. When Bond trails Auric Goldfinger to

Geneva, he relaxes with a tot of Enzian, "the firewater distilled from gentian," which is the root of an Alpine wildflower. In the Athens airport, he knocks back Ouzo; in Turkey, it's Raki. At the Saratoga racetrack, the secret agent blends in with the thoroughbred set by drinking Old-Fashioneds and "Bourbon and Branch" (i.e., whiskey and water). When Bond goes out to lunch in London, he orders up a Black Velvet, one of the most distinctively British mixed drinks. Equal parts Champagne and Guinness stout, a Black Velvet might sound awful in concept, but proves to be startlingly good in the drinking—I find it tastes curiously and deliciously like hard cider.

BLACK VELVET

1/2 Champagne
1/2 Guinness stout

Pour equal parts Champagne and stout into a tall beer glass.

Which isn't to say that 007 always bows to local custom. In *Casino Royale*, James Bond for the first and only time tries his hand inventing a drink, a "special martini." He specifies to the barman, "Three measures of Gordon's, one of vodka, half a measure of Kina Lillet. Shake it very well until it's ice-cold, then add a large thin slice of lemon peel. Got it?" Later, he names it a "Vesper," in honor of his doomed love-interest, fellow British agent Vesper Lynd. When Bond finds out she'd been working for the Russkies, the cocktail is as dead to him as the girl.

Remarkably, when *Casino Royale* was finally made into a movie in 2006, the producers managed to find a worthy new Bond; and even more shockingly, rather than stick with the franchise's Vodkatini fetish, they actually included the Vesper as a key part of the film's plot.

The Vesper, however, is not without controversy. No less a worthy than the great post-war British novelist Kingsley Amis declares the Vesper to be one of Fleming's only missteps in the drinking department. Amis was a connoisseur both of drinks and of the Bond books, authoring two books on drinking and a small, semi-scholarly musing on 007 called *The James Bond Dossier*. Amis was also the first (and best) ghostwriter to pen a Bond novel after Fleming kicked. So we must take it seriously when Amis denounces Fleming's Vesper recipe as "the great Martini enormity."

"Kina Lillet is, or was, the name of a wine apéritif flavored, I'm assured, with quinine and not at all nice," Amis writes in his *Dossier*. "I've never drunk it myself and don't intend to, especially as part of a Martini." The best Amis can figure is that Fleming must have meant for Bond to specify the vermouth made by the Lillet firm, as opposed to the company's signature apéritif.

It's a shame Amis never gave Lillet a chance. (It's usually a good idea to taste a drink before proclaiming it to be nasty.) Lillet Blanc, as the white-wine version of the apéritif is now known, is delightful on its own (if a bit sweet), and absolutely spot-on in the Vesper. With vermouth instead of Lillet, the drink is just a hybrid gin-vodka Martini, hardly warranting Bond's confidence that "my cocktail will now be drunk all over the world." But with Lillet, the Vesper does have a unique and appealing taste.

It's also worth noting that Bond was hardly the first to use Lillet in a cocktail with gin. A classic 1920s drink called the Corpse Reviver #2 combined equal parts gin, Lillet, Cointreau, and lemon juice, finished with a couple of drops of Ricard.

VESPER

3 oz gin
1 oz vodka
½ oz Lillet Blanc

Shake over ice and strain into a Martini glass. Garnish with "a large, thin slice of lemon peel."

Even with all these worldly drink choices to try, no doubt many Bond stalwarts will still want to stick with the talismanic Vodka Martini. Ask for a Vodka Martini these days, and chances are the drink will have little or no vermouth, which just won't do. Bond liked to be able to taste the vermouth, and had his preferred ratio of vodka to vermouth at the ready: "I hope I've made it right," says Solitaire in *Live and Let Die*, mixing Vodka Martinis for herself and a battered Bond. "Six to one sounds terribly strong." Well, it sounds right to me, and whereas I prefer an olive in a gin Martini, it is in the Vodka version that a twist of lemon peel works magic.

Thus we have Martinis and Vodka Martinis, but what of the dizzying variety of pretenders that have usurped that cocktail honorific in recent years? The distinguishing characteristic of the modern bar has been the surfeit of "Martinis" that aren't Martinis—those candy-colored cocktails with labels like "Raspberry Martini" or "Apple-tini" that fill out the inevitable "Martini List." For the purists, it's bad enough that a drink of vodka and vermouth is referred to as a Martini. But one doesn't have to be a stickler to realize that a drink of vodka, sweet liqueur, and fruit juice is not a Martini.

Some linguists might contradict that assertion. It has, after all, become common usage to refer to any drink in a stemmed cocktail glass—a "Martini glass"—as a "Martini." And usage is usage. The compilers of dictionaries struggle endlessly with the prescriptive/descriptive question: Do they document the way language is actually used, or do they present language as it *should* be used? The prescriptivists are usually engaged in a fighting retreat—even dear old Fowler's succumbs to new editions every now and then. Though the transformed meaning of "Martini" may be regrettable, it is an evolution no more dramatic than that which altered the word "cocktail" itself.

When the Cocktail first turned up a little over 200 years ago, it wasn't a category of drink, but a specific quaff—liquor, sugar, water, and bitters. One could have a Brandy Cocktail, a Whiskey Cocktail, or another variation based on the spirit used, but that was the full extent of the word's elasticity. It wasn't until after the Civil War that the term "Cocktail" started to be used for a class of mixed drinks—those with bitters. By the teens, just about any mixed drink served as a pre-prandial was considered a "cocktail," bitters or no. By the time Prohibition was shown the door, a "cocktail" had come to mean any mixed drink at all. Now, the word is applied, by metaphorical extension, to anything that is mixed. If the term "Martini" stretches as expansively as "cocktail" has already done, some day we will refer to treatment methods of difficult diseases involving combinations of medicines as "drug Martinis."

What a shame that would be. Though hardly the purest of the purists, I am firmly of the belief that a Martini is a drink of dry gin and dry vermouth. No other drink has what songwriter Frank Loesser calls the "slam, bang, tang" of the original. But beyond my unshakable fidelity to the basic ingredients of the Martini, I must admit a tendency to apostasy. For example, the olive or three I prefer is anathema to the most orthodox, who insist a twist of lemon peel is the only acceptable Martini garnish. Even more heretically, every now and then I like to doctor Martinis with a smidge of liqueur.

Let's remember that the classic dry Martini wasn't always so pure. It was common well into the 1930s to douse one's "Dry" with a dash or two of orange bitters. Perhaps the most common variant on the Martini was to mix it with absinthe. In F. Scott Fitzgerald's *The Beautiful and Damned*, this is just the sort of drink that the aristocratic Anthony Patch serves up to Geraldine, the movie house usherette, when he invites her up to his apartment for some petting of the heavy sort. "He wheeled out the little rolling-table that held his supply of liquor, selecting vermouth, gin, and absinthe for a proper stimulant."

Nonetheless, I think we should make it clear that any cocktail that varies from the strict Martini paradigm is no Martini, but rather a drink of some other name altogether. Thus, we can enjoy the occasional permutation on the Martini theme without contributing to the linguistic erosion of the Martini.

Take the house cocktail served at London's Savoy Hotel in the 1920's. Made of dry gin, dry vermouth, and a little mellowing Dubonnet, the Savoy Hotel Special is a fine, sophisticated drink, and one that might appeal to those who like the idea of a Martini but who find gin and vermouth alone to be a bit demanding. The Savoy Hotel Special is an admirable drink that shares the Martini's basic DNA, but it is nonetheless *not* a Martini. It is its own drink, with its own name.

SAVOY HOTEL SPECIAL

2 oz gin
½ oz dry vermouth
½ oz Dubonnet (red)

*Shake with ice and strain into a stemmed cocktail glass.
Garnish with a twist of orange peel.*

In the same spirit, David Embury allows "occasional interesting variations in your Martinis," but each variation he suggests comes with a name attached. Add a couple of dashes of orange curaçao to a Martini, and you have a Flying Dutchman. If instead you add a touch of the herbal French liqueur Chartreuse, the drink is called a Nome. A dash of crème de cassis gives you an International. Embury is so serious (or is obsessive the right word?) about correct Martini nomenclature that he insists a Martini is not worthy of the name if it has not been stirred: "If you shake the Martini, it becomes a Bradford."

Pace Embury, I give you dispensation to shake your Martinis if you like—the shaker's turbidity will not magically transubstantiate a Martini into something that is not a Martini. But if you would have a Martini properly so-called, please refrain from non-canonical variations. And remember—don't forget the vermouth.

3

STRAIGHT UP

THE MARTINI HAS HAD A LONG AND WELL-DESERVED RUN AS THE KING of cocktails. But back in the teens and twenties, the Bronx—a mix of gin, orange juice, sweet vermouth, and dry vermouth—rivaled the Martini for popularity. Now the Bronx is probably the most famous cocktail that no one knows; in the thirties, it was still one leg of the basic cocktail tripod. The first time we see William Powell in the 1934 film *The Thin Man*, he's educating a nightclub's bartenders on the proper way to shake cocktails: "Always have rhythm in your shaking," Powell tells them. "Now, a Manhattan you shake to fox-trot time, a Bronx to two-step time, a dry Martini you always shake to waltz time."

When W.E.B. Dubois wanted to draw a caricature of a "gentle-man" in his 1940 book *Dusk of Dawn*, he described the man as having "good manners, Oxford accent, and Brooks Brothers to-order clothes. He plays keen golf, smokes a rare weed, and knows a Bronx cocktail from a Manhattan."

In 1911, President William Howard Taft traveled west. He was excoriated by the teetotal crowd for attending a brunch in St. Louis at which Bronx cocktails were served. The *New York Times* in turn excoriated Missourians for being ignorant of mixology: "Mixed drinks being a part of our social system, we should know mixed drinks, if we care to be thought cultured," the *Times* lectured. "One preacher"—who clearly didn't know a Bronx from a Manhattan— "declared that a Bronx cocktail contains whisky." It would seem that the culture wars are nothing new.

The Bronx wasn't just famous; it was infamous. During the First World War, a young lieutenant stationed in Massachusetts named Bill Wilson was invited to a party for servicemen that was held at a Newport mansion. Wilson felt awkward and ill at ease at the society to-do until a pretty girl handed him a Bronx cocktail. It was the first real drink he had ever had, and he found that "it tasted wonderful, sweet, and airy at the same time." After the second Bronx, his social jitters had melted away: "My gaucheries and ineptitudes magically disappeared." The way Wilson saw it, "I had found the elixir of life." But that's too much to expect of a cocktail, and Wilson was soon drinking too many of them. Some 20 besotted years later, he would go on to found Alcoholics Anonymous.

Ironically, legend has it that the Bronx was invented by a bartender who was a teetotaler. Johnnie Solon came to the bar at the Waldorf Hotel around 1899 looking for a job. "Johnnie had never poured a drink or mixed one," Albert Stevens Crockett writes in his 1931 reminiscence *Old Waldorf Bar Days*." But "soon it developed that he had a real flair for symphonic composition." Solon managed to create his symphonies laboring under a handicap akin to the deafness that plagued Beethoven: he didn't put booze to his lips.

The Bronx was no exception. Just about 100 years ago, the head waiter of the Waldorf's Empire Room restaurant came up to Solon at the bar with a challenge: "Why don't you get up a new cocktail? I have a customer who says you can't do it." Johnnie had been in the middle of whipping up a Duplex, which is equal parts French and Italian vermouth, shaken with orange peel. On the spot, he improvised on the Duplex theme, substituting orange juice for the rind, diminishing the importance of the vermouths and adding gin to the mix. "I didn't taste it myself," Solon told Albert Stevens Crockett. Instead, he handed it to the head waiter, who "tasted it. Then he swallowed it whole." Solon promptly named it the Bronx—not after the borough or the river, but after the zoo, which he had visited earlier in the week.

At least that's the way Crockett tells it. Considering that he was the Waldorf-Astoria's PR flack for years, his account is not exactly disinterested. More than one saloon has claimed bragging rights to the Bronx, among them a pair of borough cafés. A couple of years after Crockett credited the Waldorf-Astoria's Solon, another book— Magnus Bredenbek's *What Shall We Drink?*—gave the nod to Joseph Sormani, who owned an eponymous Bronx restaurant. When the restaurateur died in 1947 at age 83, *The New York Times* repeated the claim: Sormani "was said to have originated the Bronx cocktail." Note that the obituary writer used a construction that signaled he wasn't about to endorse the attribution. Other contenders included Billy Gibson's Criterion Restaurant on East 149th Street and a no-name saloon at 887 Brook Avenue that succumbed to Prohibition (in 1921, the building was auctioned off for $10). The true origin of the

Bronx "is quite unknown to science," H.L. Mencken once wrote. "All that is known is that it preceded the *Bronx Cheer*."

The Bronx cheer still comes naturally to five-year-olds everywhere, but the Bronx cocktail has fallen into disuse and obscurity. Ask most any bartender these days for a Bronx cocktail and he's likely to stare blankly, shrug, or go digging for a recipe book under the counter. How remarkable, given how folks used to fight over its paternity. And it's also a shame, because the Bronx is a fine and refreshing drink, and it's robust enough to have spawned a slew of other solid cocktails.

BRONX COCKTAIL

1½ oz gin
1 oz orange juice
¼ oz dry vermouth
¼ oz sweet vermouth

Shake with ice and strain into a cocktail glass.
Garnish with a slice of orange.

Add a dash of Angostura bitters to the shaker and you have an Income Tax Cocktail, which seems to have been born in the late 1920s at the American Bar in London's Savoy Hotel. My best guess about the name given the Bronx with bitters? Well, the Bronx was a rich man's drink, and what could be a more bitter addition to his cup than the income tax?

Once you've added the bitters to the Bronx, there are still other cocktails to be had merely by adjusting the proportions of the basic ingredients. Equalize the vermouth and orange juice and you have a One-of-Mine cocktail or a Maurice. With a little more gin and a little less orange juice, you get a Smiler.

If it seems odd that one of the basic drinks in the cocktail repertoire was invented by a non-drinker, perhaps even stranger is the story of the Ward Eight, a classic created in honor of a teetotaler, Martin Lomasney. Legend has it that on the eve of Lomasney's election to the Massachusetts Senate in 1898, a group of his friends gathered at the Locke-Ober Café, located not far from the Massachusetts State House, and called on the bartender to create a new cocktail in his honor. Bartender Tom Hussion is said to have put together whiskey, lemon juice, orange juice and grenadine, naming it a Ward Eight, after the old West End Boston neighborhood where Lomasney was the resident fixer.

The legend can't be right, it turns out, because Lomasney didn't run for anything in 1898. Either the drink got its start in 1896, when the Ward Eight boss made a successful bid for the state Senate, or if created in 1898 it was to toast something other than a Lomasney candidacy. My guess is that it is the latter. For starters, Lomasney's win was so perfectly predictable as to be utterly unremarkable—hardly the sort of event to inspire the creation of a cocktail. By contrast, the strange Boston politics of 1898 were just crazy enough to call for a liquid commemoration.

In that year, Boston Democrats suffered a dramatic schism; the nominating convention, held in the Charlestown neighborhood, was split in two. Lomasney's faction drew up nomination papers for their man, and Mayor Josiah Quincy's crowd did the same for their candidate. Two messengers were sent racing—first across Boston Harbor by ferry and then through the streets of Boston on bicycle—in a mad dash to deliver and file the nominating papers. Lomasney's man got there first, which put his candidate on the ballot. I like to

think that this rather fantastical victory was the cause for the cele-
bratory drink.

Not that Lomasney was there for the cocktail. Not only didn't he
drink, he didn't frequent the Locke-Ober Café, with its lobster and
fancy French sauces. He preferred to eat applesauce on crackers,
washed down with endless pots of tea. Most days he could be found
sitting in his center of operations, a social hall called the Hendricks
Club, wearing a signature straw hat and greeting an endless stream of
supplicants.

One of the great political bosses of the gilded age of political bosses, Martin Lomasney didn't like to be called a boss: "A boss gives
orders. I don't," Lomasney once explained. "When I want anything
done, I ask for it." Lomasney and his machine didn't tell the voters
how to vote: "We just suggest."

Most of the time, these were suggestions that couldn't be refused.
"Martin Lomasney kept little notebooks in which he kept everyone's
name for whom he had done a favor," says Peter Drummey, a librari-
an at the Massachusetts Historical Society. If someone needed a favor
that Lomasney couldn't himself deliver, he turned to his notebooks to
find someone in his debt who could help out. But Lomasney's
machine was more than just a favor factory. The "Czar of Ward Eight"
also kept a rather large safe in which he archived ruinous dirt on
friends and enemies alike. When favors weren't enough to get his way,
coercion kicked in.

"The Boston Mahatma," as Lomasney was also known, kept his
machine going from the 1880s until his death in 1933. But a version of
the cocktail named for Lomasney's power base lives on at the Locke-
Ober. Bartender Skip Koch is "a newcomer" at the restaurant—"I've

only been here 17 years." He learned to make the Ward Eight cocktail "from a guy who was here for 20 years before me," The recipe handed down to him is fundamentally a Whiskey Sour dressed up with a splash of grenadine. "You take bourbon, sour mix, grenadine, shake it and get it nice and foamy," Koch says. The Locke-Ober serves the drink on the rocks in a wine glass, garnished with a maraschino cherry and a slice of orange.

Lucius Beebe, in his *Stork Club Bar Book*, gives a Ward Eight recipe that isn't far from the version employed today at the Locke-Ober. Both are served on ice and garnished with fruit. Beebe calls for the juice of half a lemon (about 1/2 ounce), four dashes of grenadine (about a teaspoon), and two ounces of rye whiskey. Using straight lemon juice as opposed to sour mix (which is made of lemon and/or lime juice, sugar and water) makes for a more tart drink; and the rye whiskey would give you more zing than the bourbon currently used at Locke-Ober.

As the Locke-Ober's Koch is quick to admit, the original drink would have been made with rye whiskey. The restaurant now uses bourbon because it "is a sweeter liquor" and therefore needs less compensatory sweetening. There's certainly nothing wrong with that. The Manhattan was originally a rye whiskey cocktail, but as rye became scarce, it naturally morphed into a bourbon drink. But rye has shouldered its way back onto the market. That means there is no longer any reason not to make rye whiskey cocktails with rye.

Aside from the question of rye versus bourbon, one other ingredient produces dissension in the Ward Eight ranks. Strangely missing from Beebe's recipe—and from the current Locke-Ober methodology too—is orange juice, an element essential to the original cocktail.

Ward Eight recipes including orange juice abound, including one from "Jimmy" of Ciro's in London around 1930, that called for five parts rye whiskey, two parts each orange and lemon juice, and one part grenadine. Crosby Gaige's 1944 *Standard Cocktail Guide* inverts the proportion of grenadine and orange juice and then adds a splash of club soda.

I've tried all these recipes, and none, I think, is quite as successful as the simple equation put forward by Bill Kelly in his 1945 book, *The Roving Bartender*. Kelly calls for one ounce of rye and a quarter ounce each of lemon juice, orange juice, and grenadine. Perhaps just as important as the proportions is how Kelly serves the drink: as a cocktail to be poured straight up. The *Savoy Cocktail Book* of 1930 also calls for the Ward Eight to be strained into a stemmed cocktail glass, and I think it is the best way to make the drink. Serving the Ward Eight in a martini glass helps distinguish it from the more commonplace Whiskey Sour, and I find that the texture of the fresh juices is thick, rich, and satisfying straight up, but quickly gets watery when diluted with ice.

WARD EIGHT

2 oz rye whiskey
½ oz fresh lemon juice
½ oz fresh orange juice
½ oz grenadine

Shake with ice and strain into a stemmed cocktail glass.

The quality of the Ward Eight depends in large measure on using freshly squeezed juices. But fresh juice does not always a better, or even a correct, cocktail make. For example, a very few drinks require a peculiar sweetened variation of lime juice—Rose's preserved lime juice—rather than the fresh variety. You need it for obscure cocktails such as the Rome Beauty and the Mustapha. Most famously, without it you can't make a Gimlet, a drink that was enough of a staple that Ernest Hemingway used it to start one of his best short stories:

"Will you have lime juice or lemon squash?" Francis Macomber asks.

"I'll have a gimlet," replies Robert Wilson, the ruddy professional hunter Macomber has hired to help him shoot animals in Africa.

"I'll have a gimlet too," says Macomber's wife, Margot. "I need something," she says—the first indication that the safari has gone wrong.

"I suppose it's the thing to do," says a defeated Macomber. "Tell him to make three gimlets."

In his over-agreeable acquiescence, Francis has revealed the nut of the story: he is a man who isn't able to stand his ground.

Writers often use drinks to quick-sketch characters, especially writers who liked cocktails as much as Hemingway. "The Short Happy Life of Francis Macomber" was one of his favorite stories, and drink populates the tale as abundantly as wild game. Macomber flees from the lime juice and lemon squash he had originally suggested as quickly as he hoofed it when faced with a charging lion. And there's the rub. As Hemingway puts it, "he was thirty-five years old, kept himself very fit, was good at court games, had a number of big-game fishing records, and had just shown himself, very publicly, to be a coward."

Macomber's ruthless wife enjoys the power that the knowledge of her husband's cowardice brings; promptly, brazenly, she cuckolds the poor fellow with Wilson. (In the movie version, the hunter is played by Gregory Peck, who according to the old poster, makes love to her "the Hemingway way!") Once Francis demonstrates he's not really a coward at all, and won't be quite so easy to manage in future, she does him far worse.

More recently, the Gimlet has enjoyed a vogue borne of the book *Julie and Julia*. Blogress Julie Powell took a year to work her way through Julia Child's recipes while soothing her frayed nerves with Vodka Gimlets on the rocks—"to my mind, the ideal cocktail," Powell swoons, "exquisitely civilized and not at all girly." After all, she points out, even tough guys like Philip Marlowe drink Gimlets.

Well, yes and no. The Gimlet—sweetened lime juice and gin—isn't exactly a hard-bitten drink; and for the most part, Raymond Chandler's detective hero is a slug-of-rye kind of guy. In *The Long Goodbye*, Marlowe is introduced to the Gimlet by Terry Lennox, an ever-so-polite Anglophile with problems. Among these problems are drink and the fact that he is married, off and on, to an heiress whose sexual morals would make Paris Hilton blush. Marlowe and Lennox are sitting in a Los Angeles bar called Victor's drinking Gimlets, but Lennox isn't completely happy with his cocktail: "What they call a Gimlet is just some lime or lemon juice and gin with a dash of sugar and bitters," he says to Marlowe. "A real Gimlet is half gin and half Rose's Lime Juice and nothing else. It beats martinis hollow."

Now, were Philip Marlowe James Bond, he would have engaged Lennox in a detailed discussion of the particulars of Gimlet construction. But that's not the hard-boiled way. Instead, Marlowe says simply, "I was never fussy about drinks."

Lennox was more right than wrong about how to make a good Gimlet—"a true Gimlet must be made with Rose's bottled lime juice," opines Esquire's 1949 *Handbook for Hosts*. Esquire correctly notes that Rose's sweetened lime juice, with its "distinct flavor—like lime candy drops" cannot be even remotely approximated by mixing fresh lime juice and sugar. Even so, and *pace* Philip Marlowe's pal, a proper Gimlet is not made from gin and Rose's alone.

Charles Baker made a science of tropics-born drinks in his *Gentleman's Companion* of 1939, and he devotes no small amount of purple verbiage to the Gimlet. He insists that the sort of Gimlet invented by Brits and popular from "Bombay down the Malabar Coast to Colombo; to Penang, Singapore, Hong Kong, and Shanghai" was properly made with "lime cordial," which he describes as "a British invention based on a similar essence to Rose's lime juice." Rose's by itself, Baker says, is just a bit too "pungent." He solves the problem by diluting it with water before mixing it with gin. Other mid-century cocktail gurus, such as "Trader" Vic Bergeron, suggested adding a bit of sugar to the drink to take the twangy edge off the Rose's.

In the years since, people aiming for a somewhat less twangy Gimlet have adopted a simpler strategy of merely boosting the ratio of gin to Rose's. The 50-50 blend favored by Terry Lennox has morphed into a four to one ratio. At those proportions, the lime juice may no longer monopolize the flavor, but it is still pucker-inducing. Julie Powell thinks four to one "is still convulsively limey," and recommends using "just the barest smidge of Rose's," together with vodka. But I think this is a mistake. Making a Gimlet with a glass of

Stolichnaya and a splash of Rose's is—to put it in Julia Child terms—like making *boeuf bourguignon* with chicken and a few drops of wine.

The virtue of the Gimlet is that it is a simple drink; with most simple drinks, the proportions (and quality) of the ingredients are crucial. That isn't to say there is any one correct recipe. As Charles Baker said, the Gimlet "is one to experiment with until the precise amount of lime cordial is found, to taste." To my taste, the best Gimlet is one made with two parts gin to one part lime cordial, with the lime cordial being made half of Rose's and half of simple (that is, sugar) syrup. Better still, mix the Rose's with the lime simple syrup made by the Sonoma Syrup Company (if you can find it).

Philip Marlowe's Gimlet-drinking routine comes to an abrupt halt when his friend's heiress wife turns up dead in her love nest and Lennox lams it south of the border. But when the shamus thinks he finally has the whole mess of who killed whom sorted out, he allows himself a sort of commemorative drink: "I drove out to Victor's with the idea of drinking a gimlet," Marlowe recounts. "But the bar was crowded and it wasn't any fun. When the barkeep I knew got around to me, he called me by name." The bartender seemed to recall how Marlowe took his drink: "You like a dash of bitters in it, don't you?"

"Not usually," Marlowe replies, "Just for tonight, two dashes of bitters."

That's the last Gimlet we see him drink. When the fugitive Lennox—transformed by a radical "plastic job" into someone unrecognizable—finally turns up, he reveals his identity by suggesting that Marlowe join him for a Gimlet. Marlowe refuses. After all (and as Francis Macomber learned the hard way), far more important than the question of *what* to drink is choosing *with whom* to drink.

GIMLET

2 oz gin
½ oz Rose's lime juice
¼ to ½ oz simple syrup (to taste)

*Shake with ice and strain into a cocktail glass. Garnish with
a thin slice of lime. The Gimlet can also be served in a short glass
on the rocks. Add a couple of dashes of bitters to the mix
and you get a drink that I think we should name a "Marlowe."*

Knowing with whom to drink is not a virtue exhibited by Vivien
Leigh in the movie version of Tennessee Williams's novel *The Roman
Spring of Mrs. Stone*. Mandolins are playing as she and Warren Beatty
sit in a terrace café in the Eternal City.

"Would you like a cocktail, signora?" Beatty asks, in the most won-
derfully preposterous Italian accent. "Negroni?"

"How did you know I like Negronis?" Leigh replies.

"First time I saw you, in your apartment, you tried one."

What was Beatty doing in her apartment? Leigh plays a superan-
nuated actress lonely after the death of her rich husband. Beatty plays
Paolo, a "Marchetta": a handsome and well-tailored young man "who
has no work or money but lives very well without them." In other
words, a gigolo. The movie is just one of a raft of '60s films about such
men—*Alfie* and *Breakfast at Tiffany's* come to mind—and by far it is the
most haut kitsch example of the genre.

Paolo's agent (whose commission is a whopping 50 percent of any
take) is a procuress called the Contessa. Played with an evil delight by
Kurt Weill's widow, Lotte Lenya, it's a role that for sheer nastymind-
edness rivals the part for which Lenya is most remembered—Rosa

Klebb, in *From Russia With Love*. The Contessa connives and cajoles, incites and insinuates. And when all else fails, she isn't above a little friendly blackmail. But that all comes later. At first she cares only to share with her friends the pleasures of Italy, such as the Negroni.

Soon Paolo is peddling the Negroni himself; one can't help but hope that Mrs. Stone might turn him down. But she takes it, and by drinking it, she seals her rather lurid fate.

The Negroni is a beautifully simple drink with a complicated undercurrent of flavor. A third each of Campari, sweet vermouth, and gin, it can either be served straight up—the way the Contessa and Mrs. Stone drink theirs—or on the rocks. Each of the drink's constituent parts is boldly flavored. But what ought to be a riot of herbs, citrus, grape, and grain ends up mysteriously balanced and harmonious. It's one of those curious bar tricks that makes cocktails so interesting— and maybe one of the reasons that the drink conveys an air of danger-ous mischief.

The Negroni is decidedly Italian, and not just because it is anchored by the essential Italian apéritif. The drink has its origin in Florence, according to a small book published in Italy a couple of years ago titled *Sulle Tracce del Conte*, which translates to "In the Footsteps of the Count." The Count in question is one Cammillo Negroni, who has long been credited with inventing the drink in the 1920s. According to author (and bartender) Luca Picchi, the attribu-tion is correct.

Count Negroni was in the habit of drinking Americanos, but he found that it didn't have enough kick. The Americano is undeniably suave and continental; in addition to being favored by James Bond at Paris cafés, W. Somerset Maugham puts the drink in the hand of his spy hero, Ashenden, too. But for all its impeccable charm, the Americano is not a potent drink. Count Negroni was at his regular watering hole in Florence, the Caffè Casoni, when he asked bartender Fosco Scarselli to bolster his Americano with gin. The drink was a success, and it soon spread to other bars in Florence, and beyond.

The Negroni is a bit obscure these days, but it is still a solid-enough standard in the cocktail canon that any bartender worthy of the title will know how to make it. Nor has the drink lost its vaguely illicit vibe—it keeps turning up in the hands of ne'er-do-wells. Don't look for any Negronis in the movie version of *Thank You for Smoking*, but in Christopher Buckley's original novel, Vodka Negronis are the drink of choice for tobacco lobbyist Nick Naylor. And just as the Contessa's Negroni seems to signal a certain corruption, Naylor's Negronis suggest an indulgent moral rot.

What is it about the Negroni that makes it such a sinister accoutrement? There is the name, which is mysterious and exotic to American ears. And then there is the deep ruby color of the drink. Not only does the Contessa drink Negronis, everything in her flat—walls, sofas, curtains, lampshades—is that same infernal Campari crimson. You could say the drink is a red flag.

I asked Buckley why he put a Negroni (well, actually, lots of Negronis) into Naylor's hand. "For the very pedestrian reason that I myself have been known to drink a Negroni or two (but never three)," the novelist responds. Nick, you see, has a tendency to delve into the third Negroni—usually with disastrously comic results.

Any reason Nick Naylor drinks Vodka Negronis rather than the gin original? "Being a Vodka Negroni man myself," Buckley says, "I like to think that it signals a certain, shall we say, suavity, refinement, *je ne sais quoi*, sophistication, to say nothing of startling good looks and abundant masculinity. Unlike those girlie-men who drink Gin Negronis."

I imagine the Count would resent that remark. Personally, I will risk Buckley's taunts and order the Gin Negroni that I prefer. As with most great drinks, the Negroni's recipe can withstand the inevitable tinkering and personalization. Scarselli and the Count may or may not have left a little of the soda water from the Americano in their recipe for the Negroni. During the 1950s, the Capriccio Restaurant in Rome served its Negronis on the rocks with a splash of seltzer. The bar at the Ritz in Paris eschewed the soda water, but added in a dash of Angostura, and then garnished the drink not only with a slice of orange but also a slice of lemon and a maraschino cherry. I think the Ritz method is overkill.

But speaking of killing, I can't imagine that Angostura or a maraschino cherry would have made any difference in the outcome for Mrs. Stone.

NEGRONI

1 oz Campari
1 oz sweet (red) vermouth
1 oz gin

*Shake with ice and strain into a cocktail glass,
or serve on the rocks in an Old-Fashioned glass. Add a splash
of seltzer if you like and garnish with orange — slice or peel.*

Queen Elizabeth II has been somewhat more fortunate than the fictional Mrs. Stone when it comes to strange men in her rooms—they have proved to be mere annoyances. During the 1990s, Buckingham Palace was a playground for pranksters. Twice in one week in 1992, the same man was caught inside the palace gates. In 1994, paraglider James Miller—better known as "Fan Man" for dropping out of the sky and into the ring of the 1993 Holyfield-Bowe title bout in Vegas wearing a fan-propelled glider—painted his naked self green and landed on the palace roof. In 1997, an escapee from an asylum found his way onto Buckingham grounds. These and other intrusions led *Daily Mirror* reporter Ryan Perry to test the supposedly improved state of the Queen's security a few years ago. He presented himself for employment at the palace with phony references and was promptly hired as a footman. Soon, he was delivering the Queen her mail, newspapers, and drinks. Her Majesty's cocktail of choice? Gin and Dubonnet.

The Dubonnet Cocktail was also the favorite of the Queen's late mother, who liked hers served on the rocks with plenty of rocks. Originally, a Dubonnet Cocktail was served straight up, like a Martini.

DUBONNET COCKTAIL

1½ oz gin
1½ oz Dubonnet (red)

Shake with ice, and strain into a cocktail glass.
Garnish with lemon peel. Or, build it on the rocks and you get
a drink we should call a "Queen Mother."

Does anyone outside the palace drink Dubonnet anymore? Someone must—it is the best-selling apéritif (admittedly not the most robust spirits category) in the U.S. Dubonnet is, like port, a fortified wine. It is aromatized, or flavored, with various herbs and fruits, the most prominent being the bitter bark of the cinchona tree—the source of quinine—which is why Dubonnet and other cinchona-flavored apéritif are called *quinquinas*.

Dubonnet is a versatile cocktail ingredient that was used liberally in the golden age of mixology. Take a Dubonnet Cocktail and add a few dashes of orange bitters and you get what was known as a Zaza. There have been those, however, who disapproved of putting the apéritif in mixed drinks. In 1911, *The New York Herald* complained that Dubonnet, a "delectable thirst quencher" when served with ice and soda water, was just the latest thing to be ruined by the craze for mixing cocktails: "Dubonnet has become transposed by American hands into a thing," the reporter wrote, "appetizing only in the matter of further drinks."

By the 1930s, Dubonnet was a favorite of the Social Register set, served straight or mixed. Stephen Birmingham, in his 1968 book *The Right People: A Portrait of the American Social Establishment*, recalled his embarrassment when—at his first society dance, decades before—he spilled a glass of Sauterne all over himself. Mortified, the next day he lamented his faux pas to a friendly dowager. She too was mortified, but for a different reason: "Do you mean they served Sauterne and not Dubonnet?" she replied. "How dreadful!"

Dubonnet is no longer an upper-crusty necessity, though as late as 1972, it was still being served, along with sherry, at Smith, Barney & Co.'s executive dining room. Nor is it as relentlessly advertised as it once was in the Francophone world. In *Brideshead Revisited*, Evelyn Waugh took note of the Dubonnet and Michelin billboards in Morocco and declared them the "staples of France." Dubonnet is less than a staple these days, and, as it turns out, it isn't even necessarily from France. Though bottles of Dubonnet sold in the U.S. proudly read *"Grand Apéritif de France,"* the wine is actually produced in Bardstown, Kentucky. Were George W. Bush a drinking man, he might rename it "Freedom Apéritif."

Brands often fall into different hands in different countries. Consider the crocodile-clad tennis shirts. For decades, they were a luxury item made by the French firm Lacoste—that is, everywhere but the States, where the trademark was held by Izod. After the Izod brand bounced around a succession of corporate conglomerates—each of which made the shirts cheaper than the last—Lacoste finally managed to buy back the U.S. rights, and the crocodile is costly once again. So how did a French product as iconic as Dubonnet find its way to the land of bourbon?

Paul Dubonnet was one of four siblings who together inherited the drinks fortune built by their grandfather. An international playboy with a striking resemblance to Fred Astaire, Paul had a falling out with his brothers in 1926 when he married Jean Nash, who was known as "the best-dressed woman in the world." Nash had earned that title by handing the fortunes of some four previous husbands over to the couturiers of Paris. The Dubonnet family was understandably shocked when Paul not only married her, but failed to get a prenup limiting her claim on his part of the family business.

One furious brother, race-car driver Andre, ran the happy couple off the road in the Bois de Boulogne; Paul climbed out of the ditch-mired limo and gave his brother a thrashing. "Andre weighs 20 pounds more than Paul," the new Madame Dubonnet proudly told the *Chicago Tribune*, "but Paul blacked his eyes, cut his lip and nose easy."

Concerned that Andre might attempt further violence, Paul hired a washed-up prizefighter, "Blink" McCluskey, as a bodyguard, and bought Jean "a handsome jewel-inlaid automatic pistol as a Christmas present."

The marriage lasted, and come World War II, Paul Dubonnet was with his American wife in New York. Imports from Nazi-controlled France were out of the question, and so in March 1942, Dubonnet began bottling the family apéritif in Philadelphia using California wines. Paul insisted that the U.S.-made wine was every bit the equal of the original: "The only reason our product was not made here many years ago," he told the *New York Times*, "was a sentimental one."

The arrangement lasted after the war, and by the 1950s, the aperitif's U.S. distributor, the Schenley liquor company, had acquired all the stock of Dubonnet's U.S. company. Several corporate reshufflings and takeovers later, Bardstown's Heaven-Hill Distilleries—makers of Evan Williams bourbon—acquired the brand in 1993. French-made Dubonnet is deeper and more port-like than the Dubonnet we know in the States, but I have to say that the last bottle I had of the French stuff was not at all up to snuff: The wine was muddy and so heavily oxidized that the color was more brown than red. So, I don't mind sticking with Kentucky Dubonnet. (Though, in all unfairness, I can't imagine I would extend the same courtesy to a "bourbon" from Marseilles.)

Given the provenance of today's Dubonnet, it is only fitting to mix it with Kentucky whiskey—preferably rye, which is spicy enough to balance the sweetness of the Dubonnet. Add some bitters, and you get a Dubonnet Manhattan. Add some Cointreau to the shaker, and some lemon and orange peel too, and you get an excellent old cocktail that's a Dandy.

DANDY COCKTAIL

1½ oz rye whiskey or bourbon
1½ oz Dubonnet (red)
½ oz Cointreau
1 dash Angostura bitters
Lemon and orange peel

Shake with ice (extra vigorous shaking will bring out the flavorful oils in the citrus peel) and strain into a cocktail glass.

Some great drinks, among them the Martini and the Manhattan, persist undimmed by the years. Some, like the Dandy, fade into obscurity. But even the most popular of drinks can disappear abruptly, as if over a cliff—especially, we'll see, if given a push.

4

ON THE ROCKS

JOHN UPDIKE KILLED THE OLD-FASHIONED.

Some entertainments can make a drink appear fashionable and fabulous—witness the Cosmopolitan fad fanned by HBO's *Sex and the City*. But it works the other way, too. In Updike's career-making 1960 novel, *Rabbit, Run*, a taste for Old-Fashioneds—a drink of whiskey, sugar, bitters and (sometimes) fruit—is portrayed as not only pathetic, but deadly.

Harry "Rabbit" Angstrom's wife, Janice, is an alcoholic, and the Old-Fashioned is her drink of choice. When she is introduced to the reader, the very name of the drink in her hand shows that she's lost her youth (as she sits there drinking, Rabbit notices how her hair is thinning). Yet it also portrays her as infantile (she slurps her Old-Fashioned while watching *The Mickey Mouse Club* on the tube). The drink seems childish because, sloppily made, it is sludgy with sugar, and Janice is nothing if not sloppy—her empties are "stained" with gritty sugar. Neatnik Rabbit is appalled by the "clutter behind him in the room—the Old-Fashioned glass, with its corrupt dregs."

As the idea forms in Rabbit's mind to leave Janice, he sees a way to escape the job he hates, in which he's trapped "to earn a living to buy sugar for her to put into her rotten old Old-Fashioneds." That's hardly an advertisement for the drink. And it gets much worse. While deep in her sugary cups one night, Janice gives their baby daughter a bath. Delirious with drink—in a passage as harrowing as it is horrible—she accidentally drowns the poor child.

A few years later, the drink had one of its last pop-culture gasps, this time a comic one. In the movie *It's a Mad, Mad, Mad, Mad World*, Jim Backus is a rich, WASPy lush with a speedy twin-engine plane. Mickey Rooney and Buddy Hackett find him passed out on a pool table at a flying club, and several eye-openers later, they compel Backus to wing them off in pursuit of buried treasure. Barely off the ground, Backus asks Rooney to mix up some Old-Fashioneds. The first two are too sweet, and Backus hands Hackett the controls. "Now I'm going to make an Old-Fashioned the old-fashioned way," Backus declares in that Locust Valley lockjaw of his, "the way dear old Dad used to."

"What if something happens?" blurts a terrified Hackett.

"What can happen to an Old-Fashioned?" Famous last words.

It hadn't been all that much earlier that the *New Yorker* called the Old-Fashioned "a national institution." That was in 1940, the year that Cole Porter's *Panama Hattie* bowed on Broadway, and a popular song from the show was "Make It Another Old-Fashioned, Please." The song is sort of saloon rhumba; in it, Ethel Merman wailed that as "one of love's new refugees," she wanted another double Old-

Fashioned. But the shtick of the song is that she's not really looking for an Old-Fashioned: "Leave out the cherry/Leave out the orange/Leave out the bitters," Merman sang, "Just make it straight rye." In other words, bring her a big glass of sugared whiskey.

The Trumans didn't even want the sugar. Their first night in the White House, Bess asked head butler Alonzo Fields for Old-Fashioneds. He made them with bourbon, a little sugar, bitters, and orange slices. Too sweet, complained Bess. He tried again, and Mrs. Truman, still unsatisfied, took her complaint to usher J.B. West, telling him that "she and the President did not care for fruit punch," according to biographer David McCullough. The next night, Fields, "his pride hurt, poured her a double bourbon on ice." The First Lady sipped and proclaimed, "Now, that's the way we like our Old-Fashioneds!"

So should we leave out the cherry and orange? The sugar? Even—heaven forbid—the bitters? The Old-Fashioned is one of those drinks that get the sticklers all worked up. The Trumans were of the rather strict school of thought that considers the cherry and the orange-slice to be abominations rendering the average Old-Fashioned—in the words of mid-century New York columnist Lucius Beebe—"a fruit-cup floating in a bath of warm whiskey." Beebe wanted no fruit cups, and found that he had to specify to bartenders that he took his Old-Fashioned "without fruit except the lemon" peel. The columnist recounted one mixer who flew into "an ecstasy of rage" and offense when Beebe asked for such an Old-Fashioned at the bar of the Drake Hotel in Chicago. "I've built Old-Fashioned cocktails these 60 years," the barkeep screamed, "and I have never yet had the perverted nastiness of mind to put fruit in an Old-Fashioned. Get out."

I suspect that Beebe might have been exaggerating just a skosh, but he did capture the fervor that animates the Old-Fashioned debate. For instance, does one add a splash of soda water to the glass or not? This small question has produced endless and impassioned quarrels, a dispute tailor-made for the blogosphere.

Just like linguists compiling dictionaries, the authors of bar books have to choose whether to take a normative, prescriptive stance or an empirical one, merely describing common practice. *The Official Mixer's Manual*, originally published by Patrick Gavin Duffy in 1934 and revised by James Beard in the mid-1950s, falls squarely into the latter tradition, making it a voice of tolerance and understanding. The book's Old-Fashioned recipe is a case in point.

Duffy-Beard say to start with sugar and bitters, and then to add ice cubes and lemon peel to the glass. Add the cherry and orange if you like, or not, and then—in an act of bold ecumenicalism—Beard's version of the text says to "fill with Whiskey, any Whiskey." And there, the author goes far wrong. Just ask F.D.R.

Franklin Delano Roosevelt is often thought of as a Martini man, and he not only liked to drink them, he took the mixing honors to himself. He would chat as he measured the gin into the shaker— often losing count, according to his private secretary, Grace Tully. Before serving, F.D.R. would take a taste, and if he happened to have got the mix just right, he would exclaim, "Yummy, that's good." But for all the Martinis the President took in hand, his favorite drink was an Old-Fashioned, and he was strict on the topic of its construction.

Tully liked an Old-Fashioned too, and one day a Cabinet official introduced her to what seemed to be a worldly and sophisticated permutation—making the drink with Scotch whisky. She soon came to prefer the drink that way; one afternoon, when her boss was in the mood for an Old-Fashioned, she made the mistake of suggesting that he try it that way too. "Silly," the President chided her. "I never heard of such a thing. It's absolutely sacrilegious."

Quite right. Tradition can be flouted only so far. Fruit or no fruit, soda or no soda: the choice is yours. But be sure to use American whiskey—bourbon or rye—if you wish to help re-establish this national institution.

OLD-FASHIONED

1 tsp sugar
2 dashes Angostura bitters
2 pieces of lemon peel
2 oz bourbon or rye whiskey
Orange slice and maraschino cherry

*Put sugar in the bottom of an old-fashioned glass
and douse with bitters. Muddle (that is, grind as with a pestle)
the sugar and bitters along with one piece of lemon peel.
A small splash of water can help dissolve the sugar.
Add bourbon, ice and stir. Garnish with orange and cherry (or don't)
and the other lemon peel. If you like, you can add
the orange and cherry to the muddling, but then remove them
and replace with fresh fruit for the garnish.
Give it a squirt of seltzer if you want, but no more.*

"Them what likes their Old-Fashioneds without sugar, without bitters, without water or seltzer, without ice, and certainly without fruit," observed the 1949 Esquire *Handbook for Hosts*, "are just too old fashioned to name their drink as 'straight whisky, please.'" Old fashioned, perhaps, but also serious about drinking. Those serious drinkers with the view that Kentucky straight whiskey is best taken straight have included some serious thinkers, including novelists Mark Twain and Walker Percy (for whom a belt of bourbon did "what the piece of cake did for Proust"). Percy, in an essay titled "Bourbon, Neat," advocated just that—or to be more blunt, he made the case for "knocking it back." This was not, as it might seem, a strategy for intoxication, as Percy believed the man who sets out "to anesthetize his cerebral cortex by ingesting ethyl alcohol" is missing the point. The novelist's goal wasn't anesthetic but aesthetic, the enjoyment to be had in "the instant of the whiskey being knocked back and the little explosion of Kentucky U.S.A. sunshine in the cavity of the nasopharynx and the hot bosky bite of Tennessee summertime."

So established is the cult of bourbon drunk straight that even the most venerable of bluegrass drinks, the Mint Julep, comes in for derision. One old Kentucky Julep recipe instructs: "Pluck the mint gently from its bed, just as the dew of the evening is about to form upon it. Select the choicer sprigs only, but do not rinse them." Last, after making up the sugar syrup and measuring out the whiskey, comes the crucial step: "Pour the whiskey into a well-frosted silver cup, *throw the other ingredients away and drink the whiskey.*"

Given the prejudice that bourbon purists harbor against cocktails, we must commend the Kentucky Bourbon Festival for its mixed-drink competition. The annual bourbon bash in Bardstown features five days of distillery tours, cooking classes, roots and country music concerts, art exhibits, train rides, and bourbon-barrel relay races.

For early risers, "Kentucky Bourbon Breakfasts" are served, with whiskey in the butter and the coffee. (Once upon a time, a Kentucky Breakfast was slang for starting the day with bourbon and nothing else.) Each year, there is a "Mixed Drink Challenge," in which local restaurants and Kentucky distillers compete to come up with cocktail that will be the featured drink of next year's festival.

In 2006, the official beverage was one with an oddly antipodal flavor—Island Mango Slush. Into the blender goes Bourbon, fresh mango and ginger, sugar, ginger ale, and ice. I can't say that it's bad, but it wants to be a rum drink. As much as I enjoy the tongue-in-cheekiness of making a Caribbean slushy with whiskey, well, it still wants to be a rum drink. And then there's the problem with the ginger: the recipe calls for fresh ginger root to be peeled, diced, and tossed into the blender. I learned that ginger root is not easily puréed: shredded slivers of the stuff made the Island Mango Slush about the only cocktail that ever sent me straight in search of floss.

Much better is 2004's official cocktail, the Bardstown Sling. Made with bourbon, triple sec, and cranberry and lime juice, the Bardstown Sling is a slight variation on a well-worked theme. The Granny, which was named after Grantland Rice, a mid-century sports columnist at the *New York Daily Mirror*, was bourbon, orange curaçao, lime juice, and orange bitters. In the 1960s, after vodka had begun its inexorable march helped along by the Ocean Spray folks peddling Sea Breezes, spirits were primarily being judged by their mixability with cranberry juice. One effort to keep bourbon contemporary was a 1963 drink called a Cranberry Cooler—whiskey, rum, and lime and cranberry juice on the rocks. Cross a Granny and Cranberry Cooler, and you get a Bardstown Sling.

The first time I mixed one up, I didn't like it. The recipe called for the juice of half a lime, and it just seemed to be too tart and too much. I played around with the proportions a bit, and tried substituting other orange liqueurs, such as Cointreau and Grand Marnier, for the triple sec. Finally, I realized that the problem was with the cranberry juice. What I had in the fridge was the "all-juice" variety of cranberry juice cocktail—that is, the kind sweetened with grape juice instead of corn syrup. It just wasn't sweet enough to counterbalance the sour of the citrus. Once I used the sort of cranberry juice that the recipe's architect must have had in mind, the drink worked beautifully.

That's a reminder that recipes are just guides that are subject to any number of variables, especially in fresh ingredients. Limes and lemons are bigger than they used to be, so when an old cocktail book calls for the juice of half a lemon, the author had in mind somewhat less juice than one gets from the modern fruit. Then there is the taste of the ingredients. Consider the century-old bourbon drink called a Strawberry Cocktail. It's awfully simple—you just squish up a bunch of strawberries, add some orange juice, shake it up with bourbon and ice, and strain it into a cocktail glass. It should be delicious, but when I first tried it, I found it to be bland. The problem, of course, was with supermarket strawberries, which bear no resemblance to the ripe and flavorful summertime produce that would have been the only fruit available when the drink was originally contrived. To get the drink right, you need farmers' market strawberries.

Or you can just throw the strawberries and orange juice away and drink the bourbon straight.

BARDSTOWN SLING

1 3/4 oz bourbon
1 oz triple sec
1 oz cranberry juice cocktail
Juice of 1/2 a lime (or less, if too tart)

Shake with ice and strain into a rocks glass with ice.
Garnish with a slice of orange and a wedge of lime.

Unlike whiskey, no one ever complains about putting gin to use in cocktails. Even when someone wants gin straight, a cocktail gets ordered—a vermouth-free Martini. Dry gin came of age in the golden era of the cocktail, and in the '30s and '40s there were more gin cocktails than any other kind. In the 1940 edition of Duffy's exhaustive *Official Mixer's Manual*, there are more than 100 pages of gin-based cocktails listed. The next-closest contenders, whiskey and brandy, each account for about 25 pages of recipes. Among those hundreds of gin drinks is the Gin Fizz, which up until mid-century was one of the country's favorite cocktails. But the drink isn't without certain hazards. Some of these inherent dangers contributed to Walker Percy's decision that whiskey straight was the best medicine.

By the time Percy wrote *Love in the Ruins* in 1971, Gin Fizzes were obscure enough to be exotic—and as such, to have an air of danger. Dr. Tom More, Percy's first-person protagonist, has a taste for Gin Fizzes, even though he knows that his allergy to the raw egg whites in the drink will punish him with hives and, given enough fizzes, life-threatening anaphylactic shock.

Percy was writing from experience. As a young man, he took a date to the bar at the New Yorker Hotel. The bartender was from New Orleans and suggested a hometown specialty—Gin Fizzes. "They were delicious," Percy recounted, and no doubt they were. Driving the girl home, he daydreamed about the lovely supper she was going to make him and the many kisses to follow. That's when the albumen kicked in: "My upper lip began to swell and little sparks of light flew past the corner of my eye like St. Elmo's fire." In half a minute, his lip had swollen out "like a shelf, like Mortimer Snerd," and his eyes had swollen shut. Kissing was "out of the question." Happily, his date happened to be a nurse; she drove him to Bellevue for a shot of epinephrine.

Percy, who would later conclude, "Anybody who monkeys around with gin and egg white deserves what he gets," wasn't the first writer to use anaphylaxis born of Gin Fizzes as a plot device. *The Tender Trap* (which was later made into a Fizz-free movie with Frank Sinatra and Debbie Reynolds) started its Broadway run in 1954. Charlie, a louse in wolf's clothing, knows that his fiancée, Julie, is allergic to eggs. To keep her from finding out that he's throwing an engagement party for his *other* fiancée, Charlie takes Julie out for Silver Fizzes. Confronted later—to be specific, under a rain of blows from Julie's purse—Charlie protests his innocence: "Who knows what's in a Silver Fizz?"

A Silver Fizz—fresh lemon and/or lime juice, sugar, egg white, gin, and some soda water—is one of a number of Gin Fizzes that include eggs. Fizzes were once a flourishing cocktail category with endless permutations: a Golden Fizz is made with egg yolk instead of egg white; a Royal Fizz uses both. Give the drink its fizz with Champagne instead of soda water, and you've got a Diamond Fizz.

The New Orleans classic version—The Ramos Gin Fizz—combines lemon juice, lime juice, sugar, egg white, cream, and orange-flower-water to create a sort of drinkable key lime pie. Though the most popular fizzes were anchored with gin, most any spirit can be worked into the routine: brandy and whiskey were standbys, and Trader Vic concocted a rum fizz with cream soda.

Why did a drink as worthy as the Fizz fall into such decline? I suspect it has less to do with the risk it poses to those allergic to eggs (and I hope you know who you are) than with the more general concern that a drink made with raw eggs is fraught with danger of salmonella contamination. "It is not, on a case-by-case basis, a grave risk," says Christopher Braden, MD, the head of the food-borne illness shop at the Centers for Disease Control (and a refreshingly non-alarmist official). The risk that a given egg is tainted with salmonella is about 1 in 20,000, and the fact that you'll be drinking alcohol is some reason to relax. According to an article in the journal *Epidemiology* a few years back, alcohol appears to provide a modest "protective effect" against salmonella. The evidence came from a wedding buffet in Spain with tainted potato salad. Just about every one of the guests who ate it got sick—except, that is, for those who were drinking alcoholic beverages. Only about half of them succumbed.

To avoid the risk altogether, one can buy pasteurized egg whites by the carton at the local supermarket. I wish I could report that this reliably safe alternative produced a fizz equal to the original, but alas, not quite. Even so, if you're prepared to put your shoulder to the shaker and work up a good thick froth, the results aren't bad at all.

Still, that's a lot of shaking—even with fresh egg, you have to give it the Jerry Lee Lewis treatment to get it just right. This is another reason the Fizz fizzled over the years: It requires too much effort by the bartender. In the Fizz's heyday, bars in New Orleans were staffed with scrums of men whose only job was the shaking of Fizzes. They worked as tag teams; when one man tuckered out, he'd pass the shaker to the next man, and so on. During the 1915 Mardi Gras, a bar called The Stag had 35 bartenders manning the shakers; according to one writer, they "nearly shook their arms off, but were still unable to keep up with the demand."

Demand for Gin Fizzes was international. A Gin Fizz is one of just a few dozen American cocktails included in an essential 1950 French cookbook, *L'Art Culinaire Francais*. This doesn't necessarily mean you could get a good Fizz in France. "I love Paris," Theodore Dreiser told an interviewer one August day in 1938, as they sat at a sidewalk café, "but I do wish the French knew how to mix American drinks." To get a decent drink, he said, you have to order the ingredients and mix it yourself.

"Ask the waiter for a Gin Fizz," Dreiser lamented, and "he'll inevitably spoil it for you with sugar or too much lemon." The interviewer, a fellow from the *Dallas Morning News* named Lon Tinkle, hailed the waiter and asked for Fizz fixings. "The garçon instinctively recoiled," Tinkle wrote, "and it was plain he didn't intend to let barbaric Americans have complete freedom in their savagery." Instead, the waiter brought out the ingredients and proceeded to ruin the drink by crushing a whole lemon into Dreiser's glass. "Wearily, the novelist yielded to the display of national pride."

SILVER GIN FIZZ

Juice of ½ a lemon
Juice of ½ a lime (optional)
1 tablespoon sugar (or less, to taste)
1 egg white
2 oz gin
Chilled soda water

*Shake juice, sugar, egg, and gin with ice. Then shake
it some more. Don't stop shaking yet. If you're using pasteurized
egg whites, keep shaking. Once you're worn out, strain
into a fizz or highball glass (don't put any ice in the glass).
Top the frothy mix with a few ounces of cold soda water.*

Neither the perceived threat of tainted albumen nor the intensive shaker labor that is required would have been enough to dim the appeal of a drink as charming as the Gin Fizz if a compelling substitute hadn't come along. That's exactly what happened: Come the 1950s, the Gin Fizz found itself displaced by a highball virtually unknown in the States before World War II—the Gin and Tonic.

The original 1934 edition of the *Official Mixer's Manual* gathered up just about every drink known to science at the time; tellingly, there is no Gin and Tonic in its pages. Five years later, a recipe for Gin and Quinine Water does turn up in Charles Baker's *The Gentleman's Companion*. But Baker wasn't cataloging American tastes: He had traveled throughout the Near and Far East to compile his work, and he subtitled the collection *An Exotic Drinking Book*.

Baker explains nicely how the antimalarial drug quinine came to be an essential highball ingredient: "Originated to Combat Fevers,

Real or Alleged, & which Later Became an Established Drink in India & the Tropical British East, & Still Later Became Accepted over Here by American Hosts Who Wanted to Impress Folk with Having Combed the Orient." Nowadays, the quinine content of tonic is negligible. But at the time, Baker warned it was a medicine not to be overdosed: "On more than one occasion we have temporarily showed aberration on this subject, with the result that our ears rang unmercifully and next day we felt like Rameses II, *réchauffé*."

As the sun set on England's empire in the early '50s, one of the few bright spots for Britain on the international stage was the ascendance of the Gin and Tonic. In October 1953, the British Treasury issued a report on the middling health of the U.K.'s exports, but the authors held up the Schweppes company's success "in persuading Americans to drink Gin and Tonic" as an example of the great things British business could accomplish.

The Gin and Tonic might never have made its breakout success if joints hadn't stopped charging Champagne prices for the tonic half of the equation. In his 1941 *Cocktail Guide and Ladies' Companion*, Crosby Gaige predicted that the drink, rather new to American palates, would only come into its own if bars would "abandon their foul practice of overcharging the customer for a bottle of tonic water"—which Gaige pointed out should cost no more than any other sort of soda. "American saloon-keepers, for reasons best known to themselves," Gaige declared, "suspect a person who orders a gin and tonic of being at the least a maharajah with pockets bulging with uncut emeralds."

The drinking of G&Ts no longer connotes great wealth, but it does still have a casual aura of upper-crustiness borne of its association with such icons of preppy style as John F. Kennedy. His immediate

Democratic predecessors may have liked their Old-Fashioneds, but JFK enjoyed Gin and Tonics enough that he drank them not only at parties, or relaxing on the Vineyard, but even when working out the details of the end of the world.

On a warm day in December 1961, Kennedy was in Bermuda meeting with British Prime Minister Harold Macmillan. The topic was how to combat the growing Soviet nuclear threat. Each leader had his own team of Strangeloves, and all were gathered for drinks before lunch. Among them was Macmillan's chief science adviser, Sir William Penney, a physicist who had built England's first nuke. Asked how many bombs Russia would need to destroy the U.K., Penney said, "It would take five or six, but to be on the safe side, let us say seven or eight, and"—just at that moment a steward passed by—"I'll have another Gin and Tonic if you would be so kind."

This statement, Arthur Schlesinger Jr. wrote in *A Thousand Days*, "uttered in one rush of breath, summed up for the Prime Minister and the President the absurdity of mankind setting about to destroy itself." For the rest of the summit, Kennedy and Macmillan used, "I'll have another Gin and Tonic, if you would be so kind," as an all-purpose punch line.

You don't have to be a nuclear scientist to enjoy a G&T. When Lucy the chimpanzee was famously learning sign language, she picked up a few other human habits as well. Jane Goodall recounted her experience meeting Lucy in the book *Through a Window*: "I watched, amazed, as she opened the refrigerator and various cupboards, found bottles and a glass, then poured herself a gin and tonic." Lucy "took the drink to the TV," and after a little channel surfing, turned off the set, "as though in disgust." Lucy had taste in drinks *and* entertainment.

There hasn't been much in the way of tonic water choice in the

States: Schweppes and Canada Dry are virtually indistinguishable, as they are cranked out at the same factory. They make for a perfectly good drink, if a bit sweet. Add enough fresh lime juice—half a lime's worth—and the highball balances out nicely. Or add a dash or two of Angostura bitters. In England, Schweppes makes a slightly different quinine soda called "Indian Tonic Water," which is somewhat less sweet than the American version. Some of the sweetness it does have comes by way of saccharine, which gives the Indian tonic a chemical aftertaste that I find off-putting (and which explains why I never quite have liked the Gin and Tonics I've had in Europe—well, that and the retrograde British habit of putting one sad and lonely cube of ice in the glass).

What about the gin? I find that the gins that make the best Martinis aren't the same ones to use when mixing with quinine water. Some gins emphasize the bright taste of citrus peel, which can over-power the drier root and bark flavors that give gin its savory bite. A citrusy gin is a problem in a Martini, but just what you're looking for in a Gin and Tonic. But in all cases, I like gin that is unapologetically gin. Some of the boutique gins to hit the market in the last few years have done their best to resemble the nothingness of vodka. I prefer the sort of gin that perfumes the room with juniper.

GIN AND TONIC

1 ½ oz unapologetic gin
4 - 6 oz tonic water
Juice of half a lime

Pour gin and tonic over ice in a highball glass.
Squeeze in fresh lime juice and stir, if you would be so kind.

You can make a Gin and Tonic with any of dozens of available gins, and any quinine water you can get your hands on, and though one drink may be better or worse than another, it's still a Gin and Tonic. Not so the Dark and Stormy, one of the few drinks that depends totally on specific brands of ingredients; in particular, it requires the distinctive taste of Gosling's Black Seal rum. There are many other excellent dark rums on the market, but mix any of them with ginger beer and you have something that doesn't quite taste like a Dark and Stormy. The same goes—to a somewhat lesser degree—for the ginger beer. There is a significant difference between Barritt's Bermuda Stone Ginger Beer and the spicier Jamaican style of the brew.

The Dark and Stormy is getting to be known in the States, mostly due to the biennial Newport-Bermuda yacht race. The crew of the winning boat is traditionally presented with a tray of Dark and Stormy highballs as they tie up their moorings. There are plenty more for the yachts that follow. Sailors enjoy the drink in Bermuda and load up on the essential ingredients before returning home.

The centennial running of the race in 2006 was no exception. A riot of flags flapped and fluttered at the Royal Bermuda Yacht Club Marina over the finishers, big and small. There were massive racing yachts, such as the New Zealand-based boat "Maximus" with a deck that seemed as large, clear, and flat as a tennis court, and little sailboats that you'd think twice about taking on a lake in foul weather. (The race, which first sailed in 1906, has a long history of preposterously dinky boats thrashing their way to Bermuda.) Up and down the marina, hundreds of boats flew an alphabet soup of signals in their riggings—and stowed cases of Gosling's Black Seal rum below deck. Well, mostly below deck: I saw one small yacht loaded so heavily with boxes of Black Seal that there wasn't room to stand at the helm.

I was introduced to the drink a few years ago by a Washington lobbyist friend who for many years bummed his way into the race, catching a berth to Bermuda with any boat he could find that needed an extra hand. He would bring home as much Gosling's and Barritt's as he could, and then he'd enjoy Dark and Stormys until the supply ran out. As the sailors' taste for Dark and Stormys has spread to stateside lubbers through word of mouth, Gosling's has improved its distribution in the U.S. and is now available in every state.

The vagaries of sailing are responsible for the very existence of Gosling's rum. In 1806, a London liquor merchant named William Gosling put his son James and a holdful of fortified wines, brandy, and whiskey onto the *Mercury*, a ship bound for Virginia. They never made it. "After 96 days of calm out in the Atlantic, the charter ran out," says Malcolm Gosling, one of the seventh generation of Goslings that run the family business today. The nearest port was St. George's in Bermuda, and that's where the captain of the *Mercury* left James and his cargo. That stretch in the doldrums turned out to be a happy accident. James found himself at a port full of British Navy ships, the officers and crew of which seemed to be suffering a drought of drink. James soon had to send for more liquor, and Gosling's was established as Bermuda's main importer of spirits.

The Goslings never did forsake their merchant roots for the business of distilling liquor themselves. Water-starved Bermuda isn't exactly a prime spot for planting the big sugarcane plantations needed for rum's raw material. The company developed a trade importing rum to the island from Barbados, Jamaica, and other West Indies locales. By the mid-nineteenth century, the Gosling family was blending those rums into its own proprietary product. They would fill Champagne empties with their "old rum" and seal the tops with the black wax that ultimately gave the brand its name.

Though Gosling's rum is Bermuda's most successful export, the island is really just a way station. Gosling Brothers even has the rums aged on other islands around the Caribbean. They are then shipped to Bermuda and blended. To meet the growing U.S. demand, the rum is then shipped in bulk to Kentucky, where Gosling's Black Seal rum is bottled.

The Dark and Stormy demands specific ingredients and resists even the most minor of permutations. When my wife Jennifer and I were last in Napa Valley, we were surprised and delighted to find a classic cocktail culture thriving in the land of the grape. Napa's many excellent restaurants boast ambitious wine lists, of course, but they also offer savvy slates of drinks. Nonetheless, that doesn't mean they always get the drinks right.

One night we ate at Bouchon, a bistro that is the little sister of the celebrated French Laundry restaurant. Jennifer was pleased not only to see a Dark and Stormy on the cocktail list, but also that the menu promised the drink was made with Gosling's Black Seal and Barritt's ginger beer. When the drink came, it looked a little pale—neither dark nor stormy enough.

It wasn't just the appearance that was off—Jennifer took one sip and put down her glass with a look of consternation. "That's awful!" she said. "It tastes like they put lime juice in it." Curious, I took the drink back to the bartender, who told me that Bouchon's recipe for a Dark and Stormy involved Gosling's, Barritt's and, yes, fresh lime juice. He happily made another, omitting the offending citrus, but I don't think he believed me that lime juice isn't just out of place in the Dark and Stormy, it also ruins the flavor.

"Lots of bars want to put their own spin on the drink," says Malcolm Gosling. You can't blame an ambitious bar chef for trying to add a fresh ingredient to what is otherwise the product of two bottles—where's the artistry in that, after all? But the original Dark and Stormy, in all its simplicity, is not a drink that benefits from tinkering. When Gosling's went to the U.S. Patent and Trademark Office to reserve rights to the name "Dark 'n' Stormy," the accompanying recipe calls for Gosling's and Barritt's on the rocks...and nothing more. Gosling does allow that a slice of lime may be added as a garnish—if one really must. But please don't squeeze the lime into the glass.

DARK AND STORMY

1½ oz Gosling's Black Seal rum
4-6 oz Barritt's ginger beer

Build on ice in a highball glass.

The Dark and Stormy requires brand-specific ingredients. Not so the Horse's Neck, which isn't even particular about the type of liquor—whiskey, rum, brandy, gin, or whatever—that is used. Perhaps that's because, more often than not, the drink doesn't call for any liquor at all.

The Horse's Neck was the Shirley Temple of its day, "the king of 'soft drinks,'" according to J.B. Kerfoot in the December 12, 1907 issue of *Life* magazine. Kerfoot was reviewing Mark Twain's *A Horse's Tale*, a book that opened with Ishmael-like import: "I am Buffalo Bill's horse." One of Twain's last stories, the book wasn't exactly his most biting work. A sentimental plea for animal rights, it might not have fared well at the hands of a snarky reviewer. But J.B. Kerfoot was not of that breed. Struggling to say something nice about Twain's book, Kerfoot latched on to an odd, extended metaphor, likening *A Horse's Tale* at length to the Horse's Neck.

A fancy non-alcoholic highball, a proper Horse's Neck includes the peel of a lemon cut into a long, unbroken spiral. The peel goes into a tall glass with one end draped over the rim. Toss in a few ice cubes and fill it with ginger ale. The Horse's Neck "dashes the fun of effervescent ginger with the pathos of lemon peel," Kerfoot wrote (laying it on a bit thick, if you ask me). Like the drink, Twain's story was "soft, but deliciously gingery, and if it surprises one into a pleasant tear or two, why, *honi soit qui mal y pense.*" Oh, brother.

As a temperance drink, I much prefer the Horse's Neck to the Shirley Temple. Years ago, my high-school French teacher took our class to a bistro to see if we had learned enough vocabulary to avoid the *rognons*. She was about to order herself a glass of wine, and then, thinking better of drinking on duty, she said, "Oh, just bring me something non-alcoholic." I've never forgotten the look of disgust on her face when the sly garçon presented her with a Shirley Temple— pink, packed with iridescent maraschinos, and topped with a dainty umbrella. By name and appearance, the Shirley Temple is a childish thing. But once upon a time, bartenders could do better; they knew how to dress up a soft drink without creating an embarrassment.

The Horse's Neck is described in a book by Rupert Hughes, an immensely popular and astonishingly prolific novelist, playwright, biographer, and silent film director who is now remembered, if at all, as a footnote in the life of his wacky nephew, Howard. In his 1915 novel *What Will People Say?*, Hughes described the drink as "that most innocent of beverages which masquerades ginger ale and a section of lemon peel under the ferocious name, the bloodthirsty and Viking-like title of 'a horse's neck'." If Hughes thought the name "Horse's Neck" suggested a ferocious blood-thirst, then it is no wonder that his prose has become so scarce. If not exactly bloodthirsty, at least the name was one that could be spoken by an adult.

The drink was a staple at drugstores, as British travel writer Ethel Alec-Tweedie discovered nearly a hundred years ago when she found refuge in a pharmacy during a rainstorm. "Now, be it understood, a drug-store is not like ours in England," Alec-Tweedie writes in *America as I Saw It: Or America Revisited*, published in 1913. "While one counter is given up to drugs, the other sells 'soft drinks.'" She suggests the two go hand in hand, that Americans "drink too many iced concoctions on the one side and require physic on the other."

Looking for someone to call her a hackney, Alec-Tweedie steps up to the "iced-drinks counter" and asks if she could get a "hansom cab." "No, ma'am," says the druggist, "but I can mix you a horse's neck." After first assuming she had been the victim of some inexplicable rudeness, Alec-Tweedie realizes that "the man thought my 'hansom cab' was a drink." Presented with a Horse's Neck instead, she mellows, declaring it to be "extremely good."

Though usually made with lemon peel, any rind would do in a pinch. Jack London wrote fondly of the Horse's Neck in his regretful "alcoholic memoir" of hard drinking, *John Barleycorn*. London explained that, at first, his "drinking was wholly a matter of companionship." With people who were drinking whiskey, he drank whiskey;

among teetotalers, he was happy to be dry. "Alcohol," London said, "was an utterly negligible question so far as I was concerned." He cites as an example one Atlantic crossing from his youth: "I chummed with an English cable operator and a younger member of a Spanish shipping firm," London recalled. "Now the only thing they drank was 'horse's neck'—a long, soft, cool drink with an apple peel or an orange peel floating in it," London wrote. "And for that whole voyage, I drank horse's necks with my two companions."

London later wished he had stuck with Horse's Necks. Not so H.L. Mencken, who in his best curmudgeonly fashion argued that the "fearsome" drinking thought to have killed London was also what "made him." In a 1924 letter to Upton Sinclair, Mencken declared, "London, sober, would have written nothing worth reading."

The Horse's Neck remained popular enough to be a reflexive fallback for Americans—particularly women—who weren't sure what to have. When Ginger Rogers and Helen Broderick arrive at a café on the Lido in the Astaire-Rogers dance pic *Top Hat*, Broderick comically struggles to get out a drink order in fractured Italian. She finally just gives up and blurts, "Two Horse's Necks!"

Well into the 1950s, the Horse's Neck was a favorite of young ladies looking to appear sophisticated on dates without losing their wits (and perhaps more) to liquor, but by then, the drink was as often as not served "with a kick." The kick was usually a jigger or two of whiskey; gin or brandy were also common. The drink—soft or hard—ultimately fell out of favor, I think, because bartenders found it to be too much trouble. "If a newspaperman at the National Press Club called for a 'Pink Lady' or a 'Horse's Neck'," United Press correspondent Harmon W. Nichols wrote in 1950, "old Frank Matera [the club's bartender] would yank off his glasses and say, 'Meet me in the hall, sir!'" Matera wasn't about to carve a long peel of lemon and arrange it in a glass just so. "Frank, who has been dishing out straight ones with water on the side for many years, doesn't cotton to fancy stuff."

Old Frank notwithstanding, I think it's worth the bother. It takes the peel of an entire lemon to cut the overpowering sweetness of today's ginger ale, whether with bourbon or without. And as befits the "king of soft drinks," no umbrellas, please.

HORSE'S NECK

1 ½ oz bourbon (or brandy, or gin, or no liquor at all)
Lemon peel
Ginger ale

Carve the peel of a lemon so it is one long, unbroken spiral.
Arrange it in a highball glass so that one end touches
the bottom of the glass and the other end is draped over the rim.
Toss a few ice cubes down inside the spiral of lemon peel.
Pour in the liquor, or don't. Fill with ginger ale.

5

LIBATION TRIBULATIONS

LIQUOR BRANDS RARELY MAKE IT INTO THE NEWS WHEN PEOPLE ARE behaving themselves. But let a rock band trash a dressing room, and The Smoking Gun website will quickly have the group's catering rider online showing what brand of booze fueled the tantrum.

When Floyd Landis failed a urine test after he won the 2006 Tour de France—lab techs found he had a suspiciously elevated testosterone level—Landis blamed the bottle: Jack Daniel's, to be particular. Landis's story was that, after badly losing one stage of the race ("bonking," in cyclist slang), he knocked back at least four glasses of the Tennessee whiskey, along with a couple of beers. In addition to a hangover, it seems elevated testosterone has been demonstrated as an aftereffect of too much drink.

Who knows if Landis was just consoling himself with the whiskey after a hard day's ride, or if he viewed Jack Daniel's as a way to get back into top form. Tour De France racers have a long history using alcohol as part of their doping routines. According to Christopher Thompson's recent history of the race, *The Tour de France: A Cultural History*, riders have chased the yellow jersey with the help of "rum, Champagne, port (sometimes mixed with egg yolks), cherry brandy, red wine, beer, and cognac." Landis's difficulties didn't hurt Jack Daniel's one bit—even though Landis soon abandoned his whiskey defense, the impression had already been sealed: Jack Daniel's has magical muscle-building properties. In any case, even if the scandal hadn't had such perversely positive implications for the Tennessee whiskey, Jack Daniel's is a mark robust enough to withstand the inevitable kerfuffles: the brand survived its mention as an exhibit in the sordid Michael Jackson trial.

Stolichnaya vodka appears to have escaped unscathed by its cameo appearance in the prosecution of former Tyco honcho Dennis Kozlowski. Stolichnaya was the liquor of choice at the notorious Sardinian bacchanal Kozlowski threw (and billed, in large part, to the company) for his wife's birthday. The choicest detail of the trial was an e-mail detailing just how the vodka was to be decanted: "Big ice sculpture of *David*, lots of shellfish and caviar at his feet. A waiter is pouring Stoli vodka into his back so it comes out his penis into a crystal glass."

Even when a drinks company has an active role in a public scandal, sales don't necessarily suffer. In August 2002, raunchy radio DJs "Opie and Anthony" had Boston Beer Company chairman Jim Koch in the studio to help with a promotion called "Sex for Sam." The contest called on couples to copulate in public places to win a trip to Boston courtesy of Samuel Adams. Instead, one pair of contestants won a trip downtown; they were arrested after they called into the radio station to proclaim they were fulfilling the contest's require-ments in a pew at St. Patrick's Cathedral in New York City. Opie and Andy found themselves out of work, but Koch succeeded in putting the fiasco behind him with an apology for his "lapse in judgment, a serious mistake." A few Boston pubs tried to organize a boycott against the beer, but it never amounted to much. And by the next February, Koch declared in a company press release: "2002 was a very good year for our Company," with "double-digit volume increases." Sales did slip a little in 2003, but Boston Beer attributed that to their sputtering light beer brand—not to any backlash against the Sam Adams sex stunt.

And then there's the drink that rocketed to fame on its associ-ation with the 20th century's first "crime of the century." The drink was a highball named after *Florodora*, a London show imported to the New York stage in 1900. The musical was all the rage for years, and would reverberate in American culture for most of the centu-ry—in no small part because of the scandalous murder the show occasioned.

Drinks have a long history in the theater. For one, they are a con-venient excuse for moving characters here and there on the stage. Take *Cat on a Hot Tin Roof*—a boozy play, admittedly. Hardly a page goes by without a stage direction instructing Maggie, Brick, or Big Daddy to cross over to the bar or go behind the bar. Drinks can help move the action in a play along, too: If it weren't for a spiked cup of wine, the Danish prince might still be trying to sort out what to do with his naughty stepfather.

In the aught years and the teens, cocktails and Broadway both flourished; and the stage provided the names for no small number of cocktails. The ladies who frequented New York's Café des Beaux Arts "insist on having new cocktails made, and they have to be named after something that is interesting" to them, Emile, the bar's maitre d', told the *New York Times* in 1913. "Usually," Emile added, that is "a new play, because that is what chiefly interests them." That season, there were cocktails such as the Xantippe, named after a show called *Believe Me, Xantippe* that is now every bit as forgotten as the drink it inspired, and the Sweetheart Cocktail, after the Victor Herbert musical *Sweethearts.* The 1894 show *Rob Roy* (a revival of which played Broadway at the same time *Sweethearts* was making its run) provided the name for the venerable drink of Scotch whisky and sweet vermouth.

Florodora was a comic trifle, but it was charged with the fresh-faced sensuality of a group of singing Gibson girls, the Florodora Sextette. In their big number, the girls were attended by six top-hatted swains crooning, "Tell Me Pretty Maiden, Are There Any More at Home Like You?"

The Florodora Girls did well for themselves, establishing a chorine career path—the marrying of millionaires—that was to become a stock theatrical gag. Marie Gamble married financier Frederic Gebhard; Frances Donnelly married a British peer, Lord Ashburton; and perhaps the most beautiful of the lot, Evelyn Nesbit, wed Harry Kendall Thaw, the playboy heir to a Pittsburgh coal fortune. It was a marriage that would lead to murder.

During *Florodora*'s run, the teenage Nesbit found herself the object of Stanford White's affections. White was New York's most famous architect—a designer of mansions for the likes of the Vanderbilts and grand public buildings, such as the 1890 iteration of

Madison Square Garden. White had a particular taste for young show girls, and a kinky Belle Époque notion of a good time: In his towering Madison Square Garden aerie, he would sit a naked Nesbit on a red velvet swing and watch her glide through the air.

A few years later, Nesbit was married to Thaw, who was none too happy when he learned about his wife's earlier frolics. On the evening of June 25, 1906, Mr. and Mrs. Thaw were attending a performance of *Mamzelle Champagne* at Madison Square Garden's rooftop theater. When they noticed Stanford White was at the show too, they got up to go. Thaw passed White on the way out, pulled a revolver from his coat, and promptly killed White with a bullet through his eye. In the sensational trials to follow, Thaw eventually succeeded in pleading derangement, and did a stint at the State Hospital for the Criminally Insane.

The Florodora cocktail was still in circulation in New York half a century later, though by then the drink was listed with the misspelling that is still common in bar books today—"Floradora." Syndicated columnist E. V. Durling ran across a "Floradora" cocktail on the menu of a Manhattan café in 1955, and made a point of correcting the error. He was right about the spelling, but then he proceeded to describe a drink—rye whiskey, lemon juice, and strawberry syrup—different in every particular from the recipe known for decades before – gin, lime juice, raspberry syrup, and ginger ale. The only updating the original formulation needs is the substitution of raspberry liqueur, or *framboise*, for the raspberry syrup: It's easier to find, and it makes for a better drink, too.

FLORODORA

1 ½ oz gin
¾ oz framboise (raspberry liqueur)
½ oz fresh lime juice
3-4 oz ginger ale

Build in a highball glass with ice. Garnish with a slice of lime and some fresh raspberries if you have them handy.

Sometimes cocktails and spirits make cameo appearances in court, and sometimes a drink is itself on trial. It was in just such an instance that, in April 1936, restaurateur Richard Nathans found himself in a New York courthouse, being grilled on the stand. "What kind of meat do you put in a chicken sandwich?" asked the lawyer for the plaintiff.

"Turkey, the same as in any other restaurant," Nathans replied.

"Then, the name by which you sell your wares to the public has very little relation to the ingredients you use?"

"Oftentimes, it has."

Nathans was not on the spot for substituting cheap filler in his restaurant. Instead, as the president of the New York Restaurant Board of Trade, he was appearing before New York Supreme Court Justice John L. Walsh to argue that other restaurants should be able to substitute whatever they like into their recipes—particularly bar recipes. The question before the court: Can you make a "Bacardi Cocktail" without using Bacardi brand rum?

In the years just after Prohibition, the "Bacardi Cocktail"—white rum, fresh lime juice, and grenadine—threatened to unseat the king of cocktails. "The famed Martini is reported to be slipping at last in popularity" and yielding to the Bacardi Cocktail, wrote *The Washington Post* in 1937. That same year, Hollywood columnist Jimmy Fidler gossiped that, according to bartenders at the Brown Derby restaurant, "Bacardi cocktails are Filmtown's favorite drink."

Pink, sweet-tart, and trendy, the Bacardi Cocktail was, as mixologist Dale DeGroff puts it, the Cosmopolitan of the 1930s. New York newspaper columnist Karl K. Kitchen also popularized a permutation—one that I prefer—called the Bacardi Special Cocktail, made by adding a little gin to the mix.

With orders for Bacardi Cocktails pouring in, it's no wonder Bacardi wanted to make sure those drink orders were filled with their rum and no other. So the Compañia Ron Bacardi picked two prominent offenders in New York City – the Barbizon-Plaza (a haut Central Park South hotel that is now the "Trump Parc") and a swanky Swedish smorgasbord called the Wivel Restaurant—and filed suit.

The bars' defense was simple: nobody in the business made Bacardi Cocktails exclusively with Bacardi. They called in bartenders from Jack Delaney's joint, the suave Stork Club, and the Westchester-Biltmore. "Most of them agreed that they use any bottle of rum handy when a customer asks for a Bacardi cocktail," *The New York Times* reported. The first round of the legal bout went to the restaurants and bars. "The plaintiff's particular brand of rum has not been shown to be essential in the public mind to the drink known as 'Bacardi cocktail,' " New York Supreme Court Justice Samuel Rosenman (whom F.D.R. nicknamed "Sammy the Rose") ruled in denying a temporary injunction that would have prohibited the Barbizon-Plaza and the Wivel from selling any drink so named.

When the case went to the full court, though, Bacardi triumphed.

"Beyond a reasonable doubt," ruled Justice John L. Walsh, a Bacardi Cocktail without Bacardi rum is a "subterfuge and a fraud."

It's still a good idea to make a Bacardi Cocktail with Bacardi (after all, it's the law). But the brand of white rum used is less important to the success of the drink than that crucial ingredient, the quality of which is usually overlooked: grenadine.

Grenadine is a sanguine syrup that was once made with a base of sugar and pomegranates. Go to a liquor store today and you're likely to find just one brand—Rose's. Look closely at the label. You'll find there is no sugar, just high fructose corn syrup. And the color comes not from pomegranates, but from red dye #40 (with a smidgen of blue dye #1 added to get the surreal hue just so). The label also informs us that the taste comes from both "natural and artificial flavors." Uncap the bottle and give it a good whiff. The dizzying bouquet of chemically synthesized fruit is immediately recognizable—Robitussin. To be fair, I should point out that at least the *color* of Rose's grenadine differs from that of the cough syrup, as Robitussin only uses red dye #40. I rather wonder what old Justice Walsh would have said of such sorry stuff passing itself off as grenadine.

Make a Bacardi Cocktail with Rose's grenadine and you get a drink that is a startling Day-Glo magenta. Or at least it *would* be startling if we hadn't all become accustomed to Rose's pushy, strident color. What is truly startling is what happens when you make a Bacardi Cocktail with honest-to-goodness grenadine, like the one made in France by Rième Boissons. Their traditional "Sirop de Grenadine" is deep ruby in the bottle, but the color softens and disperses in the shaker, producing a drink that is a gorgeous dusty rose. The taste is every bit as improved as the appearance.

Happily, Rième—which can be hard to find, but worth the effort—isn't the only brand offering delicious alternatives to the ubiquitous Rose's. The Sonoma Syrup Company makes an unbelievably thick and deeply flavorful grenadine called "Pomegranate Simple Syrup." Any liquor store that cares about quality drinks should carry both brands. Rose's sweetened lime juice may be an irreplaceable essential for a Gimlet, but there is no drink calling for grenadine that can't be improved by giving the Rose's brand the heave-ho.

I can't decide whether I prefer Sonoma Syrup's cane-sugar grenadine or Rième's beet-sugar version. Both are delicious and either will help make a Bacardi Cocktail that will show you what all the fuss was about. Because—Richard Nathans's testimony notwithstanding—you can no more make a Bacardi Cocktail with red-dyed corn syrup than you can make a chicken salad sandwich with turkey.

BACARDI SPECIAL

1½ oz Bacardi white rum
¾ oz gin
Juice of ½ a lime
2 teaspoons grenadine

Shake with ice and strain into a cocktail glass.
Garnish with lemon peel or lime.

[FOR A REGULAR BACARDI COCKTAIL, JUST DROP THE GIN.]

Over the years, the Bacardi company hasn't lost its knack for litigation. In the summer of 2006, while Fidel Castro lay indisposed with intestinal difficulties, it scored a small victory against its nemesis, the Maximo Lider.

Bacardi was born in Cuba, but its owners just managed to escape the island when Fidel came to power. It set up its new operations in Puerto Rico. Some of its competitors weren't so agile: After the revolution, the bearded ones expropriated "Havana Club" rum. Bacardi years ago bought the rights to the name from the exiled owners of the brand, and for a decade had been trying without much luck to have that deal enforced by U.S. courts and the World Trade Organization.

In the meantime, Havana Club has become one of the most popular brands in Europe and Canada. Fidel went into business with the French drinks giant Pernod-Ricard to market Havana Club everywhere but the United States, where like cigars from the island, Cuban rum is non grata. To build political support for its claimed ownership of the booming Havana Club rum, Bacardi threw no small amount of money around Washington, and for a while its efforts were championed by Tom DeLay, the House Majority Leader at the time. Supporting Bacardi was a threefer for DeLay—campaign cash and the chance to stick it to both Fidel and the French.

At last, the litigation paid off: In the summer of 2006, the U.S. Patent and Trademark Office ruled that it isn't about to protect Fidel's profits from intellectual property he nationalized. The PTO canceled Cuba's registration of "Havana Club." To solidify its claim to the Havana Club brand in the States, Bacardi rushed to market some Havana-style rum the company had aging in Puerto Rico, waiting for just such an opportunity. But what to make with that Havana Club rum? Not—at least for now—the Cuba Libré, a drink known among Miami Cubans as the "White Lie."

Instead, how about one of the drinks popular on the island in the 1920s, when "Have one in Havana" was the winter slogan of the wealthy? What were they drinking? According to *When It's Cocktail Time in Cuba*, a 1928 travelogue by the improbably named Basil Woon, they were drowning in Daiquiris and putting away pineapple juice concoctions such as the Mary Pickford. By far the most elegant of Cuba's drinks was the El Presidente, made of rum, dry vermouth, orange curaçao, and grenadine. "It is the aristocrat of cocktails," swoons Woon, "and is the one preferred by the better class of Cuban." El Presidente—with its familial resemblance to the Martini and the Manhattan—is indeed an aristocrat, a drink to be enjoyed in a white dinner jacket at the casino, not a rum punch for slurping in sandy swim togs at the beach.

The society set couldn't have been the only ones drinking El Presidentes. In February of 1930, *The Chicago Tribune* proclaimed from Havana: "The chief output of this Paris of the western hemisphere this winter is Presidente cocktails." Disciples of the drink returned to the States, where it was soon popular enough to be a test of a mixer's skill. "Bartender Louis Meyer has his chest 'way out this week," the *Washington Post* nightlife columnist Chanticleer reported in 1937. The barkeep at the Carlton Hotel had "produced an improved El Presidente cocktail. His boast is that it is the best rum drink obtainable, not excepting the West Indies." Meyer's secret recipe—"the reason for this definite cocksureness"—was the addition of falernum to the shaker. Falernum's main flavor comes from almonds, and it is the almond that gives classic "tiki" drinks their exotic island quality. But Chanticleer notwithstanding, I think El Presidente is better—more true to its aristocratic nature—without the falernum.

Nowadays, you'd be hard-pressed to find a bartender who knows how to make a Presidente at all. That's not to say that it is a forgotten cocktail. Rick Marin, the "toxic bachelor" who penned the dysphoric dating reminiscence *Cad* a couple of years ago, describes pouring plenty of El Presidentes as part of his wooing technique.

As with many drinks, there are competing claims of paternity for El Presidente. The cocktail has been attributed to a bartender named "Eddie" Woelke, who worked everywhere from the old Knickerbocker Hotel in New York to the Plaza Athénée in Paris and back in New York at the Hotel Biltmore. Come Prohibition, Woelke hoofed it to Havana, where he found gigs at the city's best boîtes, including the Casino Naçional. It is claimed that Woelke devised El Presidente in the back half of the twenties and named it after the reigning Cuban *jefe*, Gerard Machado.

But there are reasons for doubt. When Basil Woon finds Woelke behind the bar at the Sevilla Hotel in 1928, he regales us with many details of the mixer's life and art. And yet Woon doesn't mention the Presidente in his discussion of Woelke. Instead, he praises Eddie's Mint Julep, "a drink to cause any Southern gentleman to yelp the rebel yell."

It is a previous president who gets the honors in the other creation story for El Presidente—Mario Garcia Menocal. The owner of a sugar plantation, Menocal had been educated in the States and was later a hero of the war against Spain. The Cornell Alumni News—in between notices that Harrison W. Cooley ('87) "is practicing law in Oneida" and Arthur N. Gibb ('90) "is practicing architecture in Ithaca"—noted that Menocal ('88) "has taken a prominent part in the recent Cuban revolution." The Cornell alum had been promoted to General after he crept under a hut full of Spaniards and "placed a charge of dynamite under it." Menocal was elected *Presidente* in 1912 and, after his reelection in 1916, stayed in office until 1921.

It has been claimed that Menocal invented the drink himself, but more likely is the story that the cocktail was created at the "Vista Alegre"—the name of both a Havana café and a tony club in the wealthy suburbs of the onetime capital, Santiago de Cuba. The Vista Alegre Club in Santiago was just the sort of place where El Presidente might have been born. After all, El Presidente is more an American-style cocktail than a tropical drink. The Vista Alegre was a club favored by the most Americanized of Cubans. It was filled with "the smoke of Chesterfields and Camel cigarettes," Cuban novelist José Soler Puig once wrote. "Everything there was an ambiance of Miami or New York."

And in return, no small number of clubs back in the States were trying to capture the ambiance of Cuba. A Greenwich Village restaurant named El Chico is credited with bringing El Presidente—along with a variation of the Cuban *son* dance music called the rumba—to New York. But with so many Americans jaunting to Havana, Cuban cocktails didn't need a New York beachhead to spread across the country.

The classic El Presidente is made with two parts white rum to one part each dry (white) vermouth and orange curaçao, with a dash of grenadine. Sloppy Joe's, one of the most popular tourist bars in Havana's heyday, featured a Special Cocktail No. 1 that was an El Presidente with a half-ounce of fresh lime juice added. Not bad—but not as good as the original. The only room I have found for improvement on the original recipe is to increase the rum quotient slightly. Shake or stir it with ice and strain it into a stemmed cocktail glass. The liquid should have a burnished golden color; if it looks pink, you used too much grenadine.

EL PRESIDENTE

1 ½ oz light rum
½ oz dry vermouth
½ oz orange curaçao
A dash of grenadine

Shake with ice and strain into a cocktail glass.
Garnish with an orange twist.

It was Presidente Machado, by the way, who helped get Pan American Airways aloft by giving the fledgling airline exclusive rights to fly from Florida to Havana. That may explain why for years the Pan Am Clippers served a proprietary "Clipper Cocktail" that was nearly identical to the El Presidente. By the late '30s, the biggest plane in Pan Am's fleet of flying boats was the Boeing 314, and it featured a cocktail lounge at which Clipper Cocktails were mixed in silver shakers.

CLIPPER COCKTAIL

1 ½ oz golden rum
½ oz dry vermouth
1 teaspoon grenadine

Shake with ice and strain into a cocktail glass.

In the early days of air travel, cocktails were an essential part of the luxuries provided. A few years after the war, Pan Am was flying Boeing Stratocruisers, and among the plane's selling points was that it featured a downstairs cocktail lounge. Not unlike Boeing's 747s decades later, passengers got to the lounge via a spiral staircase. The idea for devoting so much space to a lounge wasn't just about pushing liquor.

Travelers were used to the freedom of roaming the decks of a ship or wandering the length of a train and found airplanes confining. The lounge gave them someplace to get up and go to; the cocktails gave them a reason to get up and go.

Cocktail lounges disappeared from most commercial planes in the jet era, but not the cocktails. Not only did people feel relatively more trapped in their seats without a lounge to go to, the endless parade of cocktail trays up and down the aisles added to the claustrophobia (and often delayed food service). People might not have minded so much if the drinks were better.

A lot of drinking goes on in the air, but not much of it is particularly good. In keeping with the dismal experience that is most air travel these days, airborne cocktails are rarely more than simple utilitarian conveniences. There is the thin plastic cup stuffed with ice, the little bottle of liquor, the can of soda, or tonic, or Bloody Mary mix. Combine, stir, drink. Snooze.

This sorry state of affairs is nothing new. Forty years ago, the *New York Times'* reigning foodie, Craig Claiborne, complained that a lack of Champagne—on what had been advertised as a "Champagne Flight"—was "Snare and Delusion No. 1." His biggest complaint about drinks in the air, however, was that "The wine and liquor service by some of them, particularly domestic flights, has at times, an almost endearing, naïve quality." In other words, the crew had no bartenderly skills whatsoever. He recounted how a young stewardess, asked for a Scotch and Soda, responded, "Soda? What kind?" as if it were a question of Pepsi or Coke. Now, there's no expectation that the flight attendants should have cocktail-mixing knowledge beyond an ability to distinguish the minis of vodka from the minis of gin and make change for their purchase.

What passengers have missed in the way of quality, they have more than made up for in quantity. It wasn't long into the jet age that passengers tired of sitting next to drunks started squawking. There were enough complaints about airborne boozing that on July 25, 1956, the House of Representatives—on a voice vote, no less—approved a bill to make commercial planes fly dry. Airlines would not have been allowed to "sell or otherwise furnish" alcohol on U.S. flights. The bill never did make it through the Senate, but its sponsor, Mississippi Rep. John Bell Williams, urged passage, arguing that stewardesses and pilots were tired of the misbehavior of soused passengers.

That misbehavior reached a nadir in 1995 with Gerard Finneran, an investment banker who gained a dubious fame for his drunken spree on United Airlines Flight 976 from Buenos Aires to JFK. When the crew exercised due discretion and cut the tanked Finneran off, he tramped up to first class, dropped his trousers and, in best harpy fashion, befouled the drinks cart. Alas, as it was an international flight, even if Rep. Williams bill had been made law, Finneran would have had drinks at his disposal.

At least old Gerard had the decency to avoid a Judeophobic tirade while on his famous bender. Actor Mel Gibson should have taken a lesson from Finneran on the finer points of public drunkenness when he was stopped for serpentine steering on a California road. Gibson admitted expressing "vitriolic and harmful words" of an anti-Semitic nature to a deputy who arrested him for drunk driving; but later, the actor declared himself befuddled by "where those vicious words came from during that drunken display." In other words—and as his friends expressed in their apologias on his behalf —it was the tequila talking, not Gibson. If so, then the tequila needs its mouth washed out with soap.

The arresting officer was detail-oriented enough to take note of the brand of tequila secreted in a brown paper bag in the front of Gibson's car—Cazadores. This doesn't always happen. When *NYPD Blue* actress Kim Delaney was nabbed for DUI in 2002 after swerving her way down the Pacific Coast Highway to her Malibu home, deputies noted only that the there was a small "empty bottle of vodka lying on the passenger's seat, in plain view." Such notoriety is more likely to boost sales than not, but it's not exactly good form to try to exploit it. The Cazadores folks (a brand owned by Bacardi, incidentally) had the sense merely to issue a sentence or two reiterating their commitment to the responsible enjoyment of their products.

My guess is that the Mel Gibson meltdown—as much as it may be an advertisement for abjuring alcohol altogether—was good for Tequila Cazadores, even though Gibson doesn't exactly fit the brand's marketing strategy. Cazadores has staked out a brand identity not as a celebrity quaff, but rather as a bottled ambassador of "the rich heritage and history of Mexico." Spreading the word have been "Las Chicas Cazadores," a troupe of attractive young Latina models who, according to Cazadores, wear "traditional costumes." (The accompanying photo of "Las Chicas" suggests that the traditional costume of Jalisco is tight jeans and snug tank tops.)

At least when it comes to cocktails, Cazadores has been promoting drinks more traditional than not. Cazadores has been encouraging a taste for Palomas and a sister drink, the Cantarito. In the U.S., the Margarita is the tequila drink of first and last resort. But far more popular in Mexico is the Paloma, a remarkably simple and refreshing drink made from tequila and grapefruit soda (such as Squirt) on ice. I think of the Paloma as the Latin answer to the Gin and Tonic. Tequila and grapefruit soda are also at the core of the Cantarito, but into the mix also goes fresh lemon juice, fresh lime juice and orange juice. Toss in a wedge of each fruit in question, and mix it all together in a tall glass with plenty of ice. If you like, first prepare the glass by rimming it with some kosher (sorry, Mel) salt.

CANTARITO

1 ½ oz tequila
½ oz fresh lemon juice
½ oz fresh lime juice
½ oz fresh orange juice
4 to 6 oz grapefruit soda (such as Squirt)
Lemon, lime, and orange wedges

Stir all together with plenty of ice in a tall glass rimmed with salt.

6

HOW SWEET IT IS

THERE ONCE WAS A TIME WHEN A MAN WAS JUDGED BY THE AUSTERITY of his Martini or the phenolic wallop of the peat in his whisky. But we live in less retrograde times, when the average American male can walk into a bar and order whatever he likes—say, an Apple Martini or a Lemon Drop—without fear of ridicule. The new cocktail lounge is a refuge from stale social stereotypes, a live-and-let-live oasis of choice.

Fat chance.

In the wake of the Cosmopolitan craze fueled by *Sex and the City*, girly drinks have become hard to escape. Perusing the gem-colored pseudo-Martinis that have crowded cocktail lists for a decade, you'd think that Ogden Nash—who penned the aphorism "Candy is dandy/But liquor is quicker"—was laboring under a false dichotomy.

As drinks menus have increasingly skewed toward female tastes, men have grown leery of experimenting with new concoctions. Guys eschew the cocktail list partly because they know what they want before they walk in the bar—an example of what Anthony Burgess called the male preference for "old pipes and torn jackets." But I also think men cling to what they know for a sense of social security—a Jack Daniel's is a safe, embarrassment-free drink, so why order anything else? Thus, a vicious circle: With men hesitant to venture onto the cocktail list, menus skew even more heavily toward female tastes.

This isn't much of a problem for women. They can choose to indulge in the saccharine offerings designed with them in mind, or opt for more serious drinks, all without reproach. Women who buck convention and drink gin Martinis or Scotch on the rocks raise no eyebrows—instead, they are rightly applauded for the sophistication of their choices. But for guys, the choice brings no small risk of social stigma: If men think that they're being judged by the drinks they order, they're right.

"There is nothing quite so disheartening for me as to see a rugged hulky man swagger in, take a seat, and grab the girly-drink menu," writes Ty Wenzel in her memoir *Behind Bars*. A fashion editor at *Cosmopolitan* before she turned her hand to bartending, Wenzel writes with dismay about any chiseled-faced man "sitting here having a melon martini." As she delivered a fruity cocktail to one such specimen, "I made it known to him that I have no regard for him as a man." And all the poor fellow wanted was a drink.

Too many of the trendy cocktails created in recent years have been either Day-Glo sugar bombs or double-chocolate-fudge-caramel-cream desserts in a glass. Part of the blame rests with liquor companies that promote alcoholic concoctions that aren't off-putting to newbie drinkers. Imagine that the biggest trend in wine for the last decade had been boxed blush wines, and you get some idea of the state of play in cocktails.

Girly drinks pose a problem for men and women both. Women get lulled into the rather limiting habit of drinking cocktails that don't taste like, well, drinks. For men, it's even worse: In their haste to avoid anything that smacks of the emasculating girly-drink taint, they deny themselves the great adventure of exploring cocktails in all their variety. Both are missing out. The recent revival of interest in classic cocktails presents a long-overdue opportunity to break out of the tyranny of the girly, giving men the freedom to order mixed drinks without shame and women the chance to order drinks worthy of grown-ups.

There are men ordering trendy drinks, but they tend to be nervous and furtive about it. As Lucy Brennan puts it, "a lot of grown men don't want to be seen with a pink-colored martini in their hand." Brennan is the owner and resident cocktail guru of Mint/820 in Portland, Ore. "I do see men having Guava Cosmos," she allows, "but they'll have it on the rocks" to disguise it.

That will never fool Frank Kelly Rich, editor of *Modern Drunkard Magazine*, a monthly tongue-in-cheek paean to the manly drinking arts. His "86 Rules of Boozing" includes this iron law: "Drink one girly drink in public, and you will forever be known as the guy who drinks girly drinks."

Rich does make an exception or two—for example, tropical drinks: Though generally sweet and fruity, "You can drink them if you're within 15 feet of a beach," Rich says, "or if you're wearing a Hawaiian shirt."

All this talk of lasses and their glasses drives Audrey Saunders crazy. Proprietor of the serious New York cocktail joint Pegu Club, she rejects the whole idea that men and women go for different sorts of cocktails. "I see women drinking a lot of sophisticated drinks," she says. True enough. The gender divide here is one of percentages, not strict sex segregation. But that doesn't mean the differences don't exist. Plenty of women like Schwarzenegger pics, and there is no shortage of men who enjoy Charlotte Brontë film adaptations; however, that doesn't mean there's no such thing as a "guy movie" or a "chick flick."

Brennan strives to include some specialty drinks on her Mint/820 bar menu that men will enjoy without embarrassment, such as the Mr. 820, which is Boodles gin shaken with rosemary (which is decidedly savory rather than sweet) and served with none of that sugared rim nonsense, thank you very much.

But there's no missing the cocktails Brennan has contrived with women in mind. Consider the Sweet Love: Kahlúa, banana-flavored rum, coffee, and whipped cream, topped with Mexican chocolate and labeled with one of the amorous monikers generally required of the genre. Brennan reports that it "is definitely the ladies' favorite after-dinner drink."

You can be pretty sure that if a cocktail's name even hints at love, it's a girly drink. The bar at the Rio Hotel in Las Vegas has its Brazilian Love Potion (light rum, strawberries, pineapple, sugar syrup, and lime juice). The cocktail menu at BLT Prime in New York features Aphrodite's Potion (Champagne, "fresh berry mélange," and blackberries). One SixtyBlue in Chicago offers L'amour (chocolate vodka, Chambord and Frangelico). And then there's just plain Amour (espresso, amaretto, brown sugar, and whipped cream) at New York's David Burke at Bloomingdale's.

Cheers, a magazine for the restaurant and bar industry, regularly does surveys to find out who is drinking what, and where. Recently, it asked Middle American men and women to list their favorite mixed drinks. The top seven male drinks were Rum and Coke, Screwdriver, Gin and Tonic, Seven and Seven, bourbon on the rocks, (Gin) Martini, and Scotch and Soda. The women's favorites? Margarita, Piña Colada, Daiquiri, Vodka and Cranberry, Cosmopolitan (but of course), Mudslide, and Sea Breeze.

It turns out that women's taste for sugary drinks is in keeping with the general female taste for sweets. "The majority of foods women crave—some 60 percent—are sweet," says Dr. Marcie Pelchat of the Monell Chemical Senses Center, a research institute in Philadelphia. "Only 40 percent of the foods men crave are sweet." Women also have a greater sensitivity—and thus aversion—to bitterness and irritants. Since alcohol is perceived as both bitter and burning, it's no wonder that many "women like a sweet masking agent," says Pelchat.

As women get older, however, they tend to kick the sugar habit. It is those of childbearing age who crave sweet things, which leads Pelchat to think "there may be a relationship between ovarian hormones and sensitivity to bitterness." There is some sense, then, in the slang "girly drink," with its imputation that these concoctions are preferred not just by women, but by *young* women.

Ever since modern American women started drinking in public about a century ago, there have been cocktails designed to appeal to them. The Café des Beaux Arts opened in Manhattan in 1913 as a bar specifically for women. The drinks the ladies ordered were not the same ones in demand at, say, the Men's Bar at the Waldorf: "The women differ from the men in this—they don't care so much about the taste of the drink as they do about the color of it," the café's owner, Louis Bustanoby, told the *New York Times*. "They want it to match the color of their costumes or the color of their eyes."

So too, today. Kim Haasarud owns Liquid Architecture, a cocktail consultancy in Los Angeles. She recently created a roster of drinks for a party being thrown by *Vagina Monologues* author Eve Ensler. The guests were almost all women, and the cocktails were conceived accordingly. Among the concoctions was a sweet, bright pink "Martini," garnished with a flower. "At any event, people spend a lot of time with a drink in their hands," says Haasarud. "It helps if the drink looks good with what they're wearing." The cocktail's name? The Vagini.

Today's Hollywood aesthetic has a way of making even the raciest of figures from the past seem demure. Take actress Jayne Mansfield, who maintained her rather improbable figure by eating just one meal a day, and every day the same meal at that—a well-done steak for dinner. It's not clear whether she kept the excess pounds off because her diet was protein-rich, or just because it dampened her enthusiasm for eating: "I really don't like meat," she told a reporter in 1961. There was one bright spot in her culinary routine: "I do like a cocktail," she said, "a Pink Lady, before dinner."

Mansfield styled herself something of a pink lady. Her Sunset Boulevard manse was pink, inside and out. Dubbed the "Pink Palace," the house even featured pink fluorescent lighting. No wonder she chose to drink Pink Ladies. And that has been a problem—though a tasty drink worthy of inclusion in the cocktail canon, the Pink Lady has found its reputation dogged by association with a dubious aesthetic—the sort of grief girly drinks come in for regularly.

Newspaper columnist Westbrook Pegler would win a Pulitzer Prize in 1941 for his articles on big labor's racketeers, and after World War II he scourged the Red menace in Hollywood. But in 1938, he took aim at the drinks that ladies were apt to order when they stepped into a bar—perhaps a Sidecar, a Honeydew, or a Brandy Alexander. To Pegler, the worst of all was the Pink Lady, which he jokingly described as a drink made of "shaving lotion, buttermilk, and strawberry extract."

There have been worse concoctions called "Pink Lady." A favorite skid row dram was once made by heating Sterno cans. When the paraffin melted, it could be separated from the alcohol, which poured off with a pinkish hue. With a wry nod to the dainty and highfalutin, hoboes called the drink "Pink Lady."

So how is the unironic drink of the same name made? In its prime, there was no shortage of competing recipes.

"Have you ever made a *'Pink Lady'*?" asked the newspaper ad copy for Fleischmann's dry gin in 1934. "It's that popular new cocktail with the white foamy top—that slips down your throat so smoothly, so quickly you hardly realize it's gone—except for the mild pleasant glow that steals over you." The Fleishmann folks turned to Freddie Roth, "chief mixologist" of New York's Roosevelt Hotel, to demonstrate how the drink is made. He used the juice of half a lime, an equal amount of grenadine, a tablespoon of sweet cream, and a generous jigger of gin. (It's worth noting, by the way, that the Fleishmann description of just how easy the Pink Lady is to drink captures the core complaint about drinks designed with women in mind—that they are made to disguise alcohol by burying it under a mountain of sugar.) Seagram's promoted its "soft-stilled" King Arthur Gin with a recipe from another New York bartender, Ray Teller. His Pink Lady called for the juice of a whole lemon, one tablespoon of grenadine, a teaspoon of cream, and gin.

Neither recipe was correct. Though it became common to use cream to approximate the milky froth of a Pink Lady, the correct construction of the cocktail calls for an egg white. And although the drink is indeed anchored with gin, that isn't the only spirit in the mix. With gin alone, the Pink Lady can hardly be distinguished from the Clover Club—gin, lemon or lime juice, grenadine, and an egg white. What made the Pink Lady distinct was the addition of American apple brandy. "Applejack" is no longer a robust spirit category, but the most venerable brand, Laird's—distilled in New Jersey since 1780—is widely available, and it is the essential ingredient in a proper Pink Lady.

Apple brandy is not to be confused with modern products like "Pucker" apple liqueur. Applejack is not sugary-sweet. Unless you have a particularly heavy hand with the grenadine, the Pink Lady turns out remarkably dry-tart, which is surprising for a cocktail so long dismissed as a girly drink.

Which leads me to believe that the Pink Lady's reputation is a function less of how the drink actually tastes than of its name. In his book *Vintage Spirits and Forgotten Cocktails*, Ted Haigh laments that because of the exaggerated femininity of its name, no self-respecting man has ever bellied up to a bar to order a Pink Lady—or at least not for himself. Haigh suggests the drink should be rechristened the "Secret Cocktail" (the "secret" being that one is actually drinking a Pink Lady).

PINK LADY

1 ½ oz gin
¾ oz applejack (apple brandy)
½ oz fresh lemon juice
¼ to ½ oz grenadine (to taste)
1 egg white

Shake with ice and strain into a stemmed cocktail glass.

Virginia Elliott probably had the Pink Lady in mind in her 1930 cocktail book, *Shake 'Em Up*, when she bemoaned the "tender young things" of her sex, who "prefer complicated pink and creamy drinks which satisfy their beastly appetite for sweets and at the same time offer an agreeable sense of sinfulness." Dry Martinis are wasted on them, she suggests: "If you have any crème de menthe or crème de cocoa about the house, make them up some kind of a mess of it and push them under the piano to suck on it."

Esquire's 1949 *Handbook for Hosts* included a pair of lists: "Something for the Girls" and "Something for the Boys." The masculine cocktails all involved whiskey; the feminine selection leaned heavily on cream, fruit juices and crème de this-and-that.

The enduring girly-drink stereotype has often been played for laughs. Take the 1998 film *Ronin*. Early on, the assembled mercenaries are checking their weapons—locking and loading with a menacing efficiency. As none knows any of the others, a certain tough-guy one-upmanship begins.

"Methods to withstand interrogation," says a sandy-haired Yorkshireman with a blunt scowl. "We were taught methods to hold out indefinitely."

"Nobody can hold out indefinitely," says Sam, played with a wary no-nonsense by Robert DeNiro. No phony bravado for him.

"Is that so," sneers the Yorkshireman.

"Yeah. Everybody has a limit. I spent some time in interrogation— once." Now Sam has their attention. "I held out as long as I could. All the stuff they tried—you just can't hold out forever. Impossible."

"How'd they finally get to you?" asks Larry, the wheelman.

"They gave me a Grasshopper."

Eyes widen as each man imagines the horrible instrument of torture it would have taken to break Sam. Finally, Larry has to know: "What's a Grasshopper?"

"Let's see," says Sam with a sly jut of the jaw. "It's two parts gin, two parts brandy, one part crème de menthe."

The recipe's wrong, but the gag is spot on. Equal parts green crème de menthe, white crème de cacao, and heavy cream, it is hard to imagine an alcoholic beverage less harrowing than a Grasshopper. Mint-chocolate-chip ice cream—the substance the Grasshopper most closely resembles—is rarely an ordeal.

Some drinks are born popular (the Manhattan); some drinks achieve popularity (the dry Martini emerged after a decades-long evolution from its sickly sweet ancestor); and some drinks have popularity thrust upon them. The Grasshopper is a case in point, a fad cooked up by marketing johnnies around 1949. The Leroux Liqueurs Company of Philadelphia only made cordials, so what better drink for them to promote than one anchored by a pair of liqueurs. Soon other liqueur companies got into the act, and the Grasshopper was made.

Sweet, creamy, and pretty, the Grasshopper quickly became an iconic girly-drink. In 1961, a 19-year-old Chicago woman named

Virginia Wantroba sued for the right to enjoy a cocktail at her local bar (observing the journalistic niceties of the day, the *Chicago Tribune* included that the young secretary was "a 5-foot-4–inch, 118 pound brunette"). Illinois had passed a law to raise the drinking age for women from 18 to 21, and Wantroba alleged that this was a blatant act of gender discrimination (even though the legal drinking age for men in Illinois was already 21) that inflicted on her an "irreparable injury." Her boss just happened to be Gerald B. Mullin, the attorney for the state's Beverage Dealer's Association. The new law, Mullin argued, interfered with her "pursuit of happiness." What particular drink was the object of Wantroba's quest for civil rights? The Grasshopper, of course.

Wantroba was on the tail end of the fad. That same year, the *New York Times* eulogized the Grasshopper as one of those drinks that "catches on for a while and then fades out."

A quarter-century later, the drink had become a sign of sham sophistication. In the 1986 Updike novel *Roger's Version*, a young woman who lives in the projects visits her divinity-school-professor uncle at Thanksgiving. Updike describes the awkward back-and-forth when he offers her a drink.

"How about a Grasshopper?" she asks.

"And *its* ingredients are—?" The professor, of course had merely meant to proffer a glass of wine.

"Oh, come on. Guess," she teases him.

The professor comes up with crème de menthe, but that's all. So she describes for him how they make the drink at her neighborhood bar, "the one down at the end of Prospect, with the burnt-out upstairs." The drink, to Updike, is shabby-fancy: "There was in her manner something of learned vulgarity." The drink had a tough-girl moxie traced "from a certain vein of American brass going back at least to the Andrews Sisters."

It's hard to find anyone with a kind word for the innocuous old orthopteran.

Embury, in *The Fine Art of Mixing Drinks*, makes clear his dislike for frothy, creamy treats, and that most certainly includes the Grasshopper. He derided it as a "so-called cocktail." Embury was a stickler that anything properly labeled a "cocktail" had to serve as a pre-prandial—a stimulant to the appetite. The Grasshopper is dessert in a glass, its sweetness and its thick heaviness making it particularly ill-suited to the role of apéritif. (It is so well suited to the end of a meal that it soon morphed into an honest-to-goodness pie, a dish that, by the late 1960s, eclipsed the drink that inspired it.)

Embury discussed various permutations on the drink: "One bar in New York City cuts down on the cream and adds blackberry brandy. This results in a rather muddy-looking locust," he sniffs. "With or without the blackberry, as a cocktail it is strictly vile."

I think that's unduly harsh. The drink is generally too sweet for me, but it is—DeNiro's Sam notwithstanding—no torture. Those who like Peppermint Patties will find the Grasshopper a pleasant way to wrap up a meal. However, I think the classic recipe could stand one simple change. Every green crème de menthe I've found is colored in that particular electric hue otherwise reserved for antifreeze. If you choose to use clear crème de cacao, the crème de menthe gives the drink a glaring lime-drop brightness. Instead, try using dark crème de cacao, and you'll get a Grasshopper dressed in a muted, Restoration Hardware-style sage green.

And even if such a sweet concoction isn't your style, remember—it's still preferable to waterboarding.

THE GRASSHOPPER

1 oz crème de menthe (green)
1 oz crème de cacao (either clear or dark)
1 oz cream (or half-and-half)

Shake with ice and strain into a saucer Champagne glass.

If the Grasshopper was the essential girly drink of the fifties, the template for the girly drinks of our times is the Cosmopolitan, which inspired a whole generation of like-minded girly-Martinis that have dominated cocktail lists for a decade. The Cosmo was invented in the mid-1980s by Cheryl Cook, a bartender in Miami's South Beach. She noticed that "women were ordering Martinis just to have a drink in that classic glass," but they didn't actually like how the drink tasted. So she set about making a drink that was "pretty, and pretty tasty too." The cocktail she came up with was citrus vodka, triple sec, Rose's lime juice, and a splash of cranberry served straight up.

The near-ubiquity of Cosmo-inspired girly drinks can make them hard to avoid. "Suave gentlemen are canvassing a menu for anything that doesn't scream *Sissy-Boy*—but can't find it," laments bartender/author Ty Wenzel.

But what of the self-respecting man who just happens to have a sweet tooth? What can he drink without risking the censorious stares of the Wenzels of the world? Perhaps his best choice is the Smith and Curran, a drink of such sweet creaminess that it would be a girly classic were it not for the highball's burly back-story.

In April of 1951, Amerada Petroleum drilled a hole into Clarence Iverson's farm eight miles south of Tioga, ND, and struck oil. News of the find spread fast, and soon there was a black-gold rush to North Dakota. The state was inundated with wildcatters, land speculators, geologists, and roughnecks. They crowded into little Tioga, where the population quintupled, to 2,700, but the biggest base of operations was Bismarck, where every inch of office space was leased, every hotel room booked, and every barstool taken.

The most popular bar with the oilmen of Bismarck was the Blue Blazer Lounge in the Prince Hotel. The bar got its name not from the brass-buttoned jacket but from a legendary drink devised a century earlier by "Professor" Jerry Thomas, author of the first real cocktail book. Thomas's Blue Blazer was a triumph of showbiz, though not exactly a lip-smacker—the ingredients are warm Scotch, boiling water, and sugar. Thomas would take two silver-plated mugs and put hot water and a teaspoon of sugar in one, and some well-heated whiskey in the other. After igniting the Scotch with a match, Thomas would toss the flaming whiskey into the other mug, and then back and forth a half-dozen times. "If well done," Thomas writes in his 1862 *Bartender's Guide*, "this will have the appearance of a continued stream of liquid fire." Thomas warned the novice "to practice for some time with cold water," so as "not to scald himself." This dangerous drink was the specialty of the Blue Blazer Lounge, but not a favorite with customers, who weren't exactly clamoring for hot whiskey and water.

Two of those customers were oilmen Wendell Smith and James Curran. Smith was a geologist who had come to North Dakota for Mobil Oil; Curran was a "land man"—a speculator who locked up drilling rights and then brokered the leases to explorers. Curran needed a good geologist to scout land, and he persuaded Smith to be his partner. "Smith and Curran" set up shop in a room on the second floor of the Grand Pacific Hotel, but they liked to do their drinking over at the Blue Blazer. It was there they created the drink that bears their names.

That is, it bears *one* of their names. By the time the highball known as the Smith and Curran became established as a standard part of the mixologist's repertoire, the name had been misheard, repeated, and passed on enough times in enough noisy bars that it was corrupted to "Smith and Kern" or "Smith and Kearns," which is the way the drink came to be listed in cocktail books.

"Smith and Curran were regular rounders," says Al Golden, a Bismarck oilman who is still active in oil exploration and who knew the two in the fifties. They spent no small amount of time in the company of the Blue Blazer's diminutive bartender, Gebert "Shorty" Doebber.

One Saturday in 1952, Smith and Curran asked Shorty to come up with a house drink that would taste better than a Blue Blazer. The two had been at the Blazer late the night before and were looking for a restorative: "They complained about how bad they felt," Golden recalls, "and asked for something to make it better." Shorty tried any number of new combinations of liquor, none of which met with Smith and Curran's approval. He finally hit on a particularly soothing concoction that was delicious, but decidedly odd as the product of an oil boom. One thinks of oilmen as a rough and tumble crowd—manly men who take their slugs from the bottle and wipe their mouths with the backs of their hands. The Smith and Curran—a chocolaty, creamy fizz of a drink—does not fit the stereotype.

Into a highball glass full of ice, Shorty poured a couple of ounces of crème de cacao. Then, he added an ounce of sweet dairy cream and enough soda water to top up the glass. A quick stir, and you have an Egg Cream with a kick.

The drink quickly became a favorite of the boom crowd. When the frenzy of drilling finally petered out, the oilmen scattered, taking their taste for Smith and Currans with them. "I've ordered it by name in Houston, Springfield, Cheyenne, Billings, and many other spots," says retired oil lobbyist Jack Swenson. "Wherever there have been oil field people around, bartenders have known the drink."

Given the peripatetic careers of oilmen, "you can go anywhere in the world and order a Smith and Curran," says Sen. Kent Conrad of North Dakota. "I've ordered that drink in Istanbul, Turkey, and the bartender knew exactly what it was without having to look it up." Sen. Conrad's taste for the drink is a sentimental one. Wendell Smith was friendly with a fellow North Dakotan, Gaylord Conrad, and his wife. When the Conrads were killed in a car crash in 1953, Smith was one of a number of their old Bismarck friends who pitched in to help support and educate the couple's orphaned children. Years later, when Smith went off to search the deserts of Libya for oil, he took one of the Conrads' sons with him—which is how Senator Conrad came to attend high school in Tripoli.

The Smith and Curran (well, at least the "Smith and Kearns") has enough of a general following that most bartenders this side of Turkey will know how to make it without benefit of a bar book. But whether they look it up or not, most bartenders get the drink wrong—somewhere along the way, not only was the name of the drink corrupted, but the recipe too, with Kahlúa replacing the crème de cacao. In the early 1980s, one Bismarck bar—clearly confused by the name of the basic ingredient—was making the Smith and Curran with curaçao instead of cacao. Asked about the variations by a reporter from the *Bismarck Tribune* in 1982, Jimmy Curran was unequivocal: "You tell them to cut that out."

SMITH AND CURRAN

2 oz crème de cacao
1 oz sweet cream (or half-and-half)
Soda water

Build over ice in a highball glass and stir just enough to mix the ingredients, but not so much as to dissipate the soda.

Even drinks that start out unfreighted by gender implications can come to be seen as feminine frills. A case in point is the near-extinct Pousse Café, a most decidedly un-mixed drink.

Kurt Vonnegut once told *Playboy* that *Slaughterhouse-Five* and *Breakfast of Champions* "used to be one book. But they separated completely. It was like a pousse-café, like oil and water—they simply were not mixable. So I was able to decant *Slaughterhouse-Five*, and what was left was *Breakfast of Champions*."

Vonnegut was a bit glib with his metaphors. A Pousse Café does indeed start out with its component parts separate and distinct. The after-dinner drink is made of liqueurs and spirits layered one on top of the other, in order of decreasing density. If done right, the crisp, varicolored strata make the glass resemble a pack of mixed-fruit Life Savers. But unlike oil and water, those components are all too mixable. Indeed, the untimely blending of Pousse Café layers was once something of a standard gag.

Take the *New York Times* story from May 1903, boldly headlined "A POUSSE CAFÉ SACRILEGE." The item even warranted a subhead: "Customer's Way of Disposing of the Drink Astounded Its Concocter." The article describes a well-dressed customer—albeit one with "an air of the provincial about him"—ambling into the Fifth Avenue Hotel bar and ordering a Pousse Café. Bartender Hugh Dame, "one of the dispensers of exhilarating concoctions," worked a quarter of an hour on an eight-layer masterpiece. "The purchaser watched the process, and when the glass was placed before him, asked for a straw." Leery, the bartender gave the man what he asked for. "As he saw the customer coolly insert it in the mixture and stir the contents of the glass, he clasped his hands to his hips and gazed in astonishment. He could not speak." The customer drained the muddy mixture, paid, and left, while Dame's apoplectic face was fixed in "a rare study for an artist."

Half a century later, the urban legend had morphed. This time, instead of featuring a bumpkin, the Pousse Café culprits were women, and the offended bartender had become more assertive. "Two couples went into a well patronized Loop bar recently," said the *Chicago Tribune* in August of 1948. "The men ordered Scotch and Sodas, and the women ordered Pousse Cafés." The bartender "labored furiously" to make "things of beauty." But his "happy look of self-satisfaction changed to one of indignation as he saw the women casually stir their drinks with their fingers." Outraged, he seized the drinks—even the men's whiskies—and poured them all down the drain, declaring, "You will be served *NO* more drinks at this bar."

Such incidents—real or fanciful—explain why, when Washington's Hi-Hat Club made Pousse Cafés a house specialty in the late thirties, it provided instructions. "If it's new to you, the manager tells you how to drink it," the *Washington Post* reported. "Certainly it's one drink that can't be swallowed by instinct."

Perhaps not, but that doesn't mean it's hard to quaff. Poet Howard Nemerov captured the correct approach in his poem *History of a Literary Movement*, in which a dead man is remembered: "I can still see him sitting there/Sipping level by level/his Pousse-café."

How many levels? The standard was six. The most extravagant effort—34 strata—is attributed to a famous mid-century New Orleans bartender named Nick Castrogiovanni; in their earliest incarnations, Pousse Cafés were simple affairs of three layers, or even just two. In 1898, the *New York Herald* described a "Pousse Café a La Montague" made of "cold, rich cream" on top of Benedictine. The rather excited reporter enthused that "the cordial comes bubbling up through the cream as a delicious, wicked suggestion might surge through the veins of an innocent maiden."

The passion for Pousse Cafés peaked in the 1890s. Citizens of a later, more streamlined era dismissed them as frou-frou affectations. In his 1939 *Gun Club Drink Book*, Charles Browne derides the Pousse Café as a drink that "used to be rather popular with sophomores visiting night clubs for the first time." A few descendents of the Pousse Café survive, such as the B-52, a layered "shooter" from the 1980s made with Kahlúa, Baileys, and Grand Marnier.

Even as the drink disappeared from mixologists' skill set, its name continued to have resonance. In 1966, *Pousse Café* served as the title for a Broadway musical featuring some of the least memorable songs Duke Ellington ever wrote. The show proved to be the sort of grand flop that Bialystock and Bloom could only dream of. More recently, there was an independent film by the same name; the dysfunctional family drama centered on a writer of bar books striving to master layering the difficult drink.

Over time, the degree of difficulty that the drink entails has been exaggerated. A three- or four-layer Pousse Café is easy enough to make, if you use liqueurs of sufficiently different "specific gravities." After the first layer is nestled in the bottom of the glass, place a spoon against the inside of the glass and slowly pour the next layer over the spoon. If you try putting a denser liqueur on top of a lighter one, you'll know it—the heavier will slip underneath, finding the spot where it belongs.

TRIPLE POUSSE CAFÉ

⅓ curaçao
⅓ Chartreuse
⅓ cognac

A recipe from the 1937 Famous New Orleans Drinks and How to Mix 'Em *by Stanley Clisby Arthur, who writes:*
"Easily made so it is suggested that the amateur mixer try his hand on this one before experimenting with the multiple-ringed kinds. It has all the delights of the more intricate pousse cafés."
Layer the spirits, starting with the curaçao, in a small, narrow glass.

Making Pousse Cafés yourself is about the only way you'll ever experience the drink. Pat O'Brien's in New Orleans still has the knack. But when I tried a few venerable New York spots rumored to know how to pour one, including Tavern on the Green and the "Bull and Bear" at the Waldorf-Astoria, I had no luck—the Tavern's bartender was confused, and the Waldorf's man couldn't be bothered.

However, there is one very modern bar that has made something of a specialty of the Pousse Café—albeit with a high-tech twist. The Below Zero Nitro Bar in Miami Beach uses liquid nitrogen to freeze the various layers in place. It's just one of their un-mixed drinks, such as the Nitro-tini: a glass of vodka with a swizzle stick made of flash-frozen vermouth and an olive turned into an instant briny ice cube.

The Nitro Bar is part of a relatively new—and not always regrettable—cocktail trend: the adaptation of circus tricks from the hyper-trendy food fad "molecular gastronomy." Practitioners combine high tech with a post-modern wink and a nod to engineer unusual food and drink, gleefully exploring textures and tastes unknown to nature. The "Minibar" at Washington's Café Atlantico is one practitioner. Its Carbonated Mojito is suspended inside a jiggling olive-drab membrane. It looked like a tiny half-deflated balloon lolling on a spoon; popped in the mouth, it bursts with convincing Mojito flavor.

Among the basic shticks in the molecular bag is deconstruction— the isolation of flavor components found in common dishes. The components can then be reassembled in curious new ways. To keep the component parts separate, the molecular chef employs gels, foams, powders, membranes made of processed algae polymers, and anything else that can be found as media or methods for flavor suspension.

Of all the molecular gastronomic gimmicks, the easiest to manage at home, and the best suited to cocktails, is foam. Any number of traditional drinks—the Silver Gin Fizz and a pint of Guinness among them—come standard with a nice, frothy foam on top. Of course, with a Gin Fizz or with stout, the foam is the same flavor as the drink. The molecular spin is to whip up a foam with a flavor separate from the taste of the liquid in the glass, allowing for the kind of deconstruction that might otherwise require liquid nitrogen.

Charlotte Voisey, a bartender schooled in the trendy London scene, uses foam in whipping up a deconstructed Negroni. She starts by altering the standard Negroni formula of gin, sweet vermouth, and Campari to gin, Lillet Blanc, and Aperol (an orangey Italian apéritif). The gin and Lillet go into a glass with ice; the Aperol goes on top in the form of a flavored foam.

To make the foam, Voisey starts with an egg white stretched with either juice or water and then intensely flavored. "Anytime you make a foam," she says, "it needs to be extreme," so the flavor comes through in the froth. The foam ingredients go in a nitrous-oxide-chargeable whipped-cream dispenser. Contrary to the manufacturer's guidelines, Voisey likes to double-charge the canister before shaking the heck out of it, and the result is a smooth, almost meringue-like foam. Using a charged dispenser lets you make your foam ahead of time and keep it at the ready, which is particularly helpful to bartenders.

At home, there's a simpler way. Just get a sturdy, wide glass and put in it all the foam's ingredients. Put a whisk in the glass and then rub its handle vigorously between your flattened palms, like a Cub Scout trying to start a fire with sticks. Soon, you'll have a well-aerated foam that can be spooned lightly onto the top of a drink.

You don't need to alter the basic parts of the Negroni to get an interesting drink. Gin and sweet vermouth on the rocks topped with a Campari foam makes for a perfectly palatable permutation on the original Negroni theme. It's also worth playing around with other classic standards. Voisey also makes a deconstructed Manhattan of whiskey and bitters topped with a sweet vermouth and maraschino foam.

That said, approach the Martini at your peril. Voisey has experimented with olive-brine foam-topped Martinis and—not surprisingly—has found them to be less than successful. "There's no room to hide with a Martini," she says. "It's got to be spot-on, or not at all."

When it comes to deconstructed Martinis, I'll take not at all.

DECONSTRUCTED NEGRONI

1½ oz gin
1½ oz Lillet Blanc

Build over ice in a short glass and stir.
Top with Aperol foam (made in separate glass).

APEROL FOAM

1 egg white
2 oz strained grapefruit juice
1 oz Aperol
2 tsp orange bitters.

Swizzle-whisk ingredients into a frothy foam.

You don't have to flirt with high-tech culinary gimmicks to achieve a foam-topped, deconstructed drink. One of the great classics—Irish Coffee—pioneered the concept. A true Irish Coffee is delicious and one of the few sweet, cream-enhanced drinks that has largely escaped the "girly drink" taint. But why? Perhaps because the coffee is spiked with that least feminine-seeming of spirits, whiskey. Or perhaps it is because sugar and cream are perfectly natural additions to coffee, even if one is a man—which I find revealing about the prejudices underpinning the derision of "ladies' drinks." The very qualities—sweetness, creaminess—that mark an alcoholic beverage as girly are not thought the least bit unmanly when it comes to food or non-alcoholic drink. Booze free from frills may be an essential tough-guy accessory, but dessert is not similarly loaded with meaning.

So who gets the credit for inventing that rare cup that speaks equally to men and women? Of all the classic drinks, few have a provenance quite so clearly established and widely promulgated as the story behind Irish Coffee—and it just might be a fraud.

The story goes like this: In 1942, Joe Sheridan took a job as chef at the Foynes (later named Shannon) Airport, where transatlantic flying boats docked in Ireland. He was tasked with creating a drink to warm up passengers chilled from their flights, and promptly put together black coffee, Irish whiskey, and sugar in a goblet and topped it with a thick layer of heavy cream. According to the official "History of Irish Coffee" at the Foynes Flying Boat Museum, "a surprised American passenger asked, 'Is this Brazilian coffee?' 'No,' Joe said, 'That's Irish Coffee.'"

Let's give Sheridan his due. He is no doubt responsible for bringing Irish Coffee to the attention of a globetrotting crowd. But perhaps—and I realize that to suggest this risks committing a heresy not unlike claiming that the Earl of Oxford was the real scribbler behind Hamlet and the rest—Sheridan did not actually invent the drink.

The contrarian account can be found buried in an essay by John V. Kelleher, a professor of Irish Studies at Harvard from 1952 to 1986. Just after World War II, Kelleher visited Ireland, and some literary pals took him to the pub at a hotel called The Dolphin in Dublin's

Temple Bar neighborhood. (The Dolphin is still standing, but it is now an office building.) "The Dolphin, I was told, was where Irish coffee had been invented," Kelleher later wrote. "The proprietor, Michael Nugent, had concocted it during the War as a way of disguising what was then called coffee." When Kelleher stopped by in 1946, the "chief merit" of the Dolphin's Irish Coffee "was the interesting difficulty of floating the cream onto but not into the liquid."

There is reason to credit the claim centered on the Dolphin. Kelleher was a serious scholar who was unlikely to cite any and every bit of self-promotion floated by a publican. Beyond that, the story is credible. Think about the Foynes/Shannon Airport version: If you were trying to warm up chilled passengers by spiking coffee, wouldn't a rather traditional approach of dropping sugar and whiskey in the coffee be enough to do the trick? On the other hand, if you were trying to mask the taste of dreadful wartime coffee, you might go the extra distance and dress it up with a thick layer of cream on top.

Then there's the timeline: Joe Sheridan is said to have invented Irish Coffee soon after taking his new job at the airport in 1942. Before he went to Foynes, Sheridan worked at a department store in Dublin that was a short walk from the Dolphin. Sheridan would have had ample opportunity to pop in at the Dolphin and sample Michael Nugent's creation.

There's one last reason to prefer the revisionist version focused on the Dolphin. If the airport is really where Irish Coffee got its start, then the drink isn't much more Gaelic than, say, French Toast is Gallic. Yes, it uses key local ingredients—whiskey and cream. And if made correctly, Irish Coffee has an uncanny resemblance to a well-poured Guinness. But a concoction fashioned exclusively for international travelers isn't exactly Irish, at least not the way soda bread is. In 1962, Dublin's Lord Mayor, Robert Briscoe, visited Washington and sniffed at Irish Coffee: "It's too sweet for me," he told reporters. "I prefer my Jameson neat." However, if Irish Coffee was indeed born at the Dolphin—a pub that was enough of a Dublin landmark to get a mention in *Ulysses*—then the drink's Irish bona fides are unimpeachable.

The other half of the Irish Coffee story—how the drink immigrated to America—is also in need of revision. Legend has it that Irish Coffee was introduced to the U.S. at the Buena Vista, a restaurant and bar at Fisherman's Wharf in San Francisco. In 1952, travel writer Stanton Delaplane and restaurateur Jack Koeppler tried to recreate the drink they'd had at the Shannon airport. Frustrated with their failed attempts—especially the problem of sinking cream—Koeppler flew to Shannon to learn the trick of the thing from Joe Sheridan himself. Recipe in hand, and with the help of some promotional copy by Delaplane, Koeppler turned the Buena Vista into an Irish Coffee factory. At one point the restaurant accounted for some 10 percent of the nation's consumption of Irish whiskey.

Though the Buena Vista can rightly claim credit for having popularized Irish Coffee in America, the bar is not where the drink was first introduced in the States. That credit goes to the delightfully named Clementine Paddleford, for years the popular and influential food writer for the *New York Herald Tribune*. On St. Patrick's Day in 1948, Paddleford suggested that her readers try Irish Coffee, "the traditional Gaelic drink as served to passengers in the lounge at Shannon Airport." She thanked Pan American air hostess Maureen Grogan for getting her the recipe: "Place two tablespoons of Irish whiskey in a warm glass, add one teaspoon sugar, pour in the hot coffee, and float two inches of whipped cream," Paddleford wrote. "Sip and the whiskey laces through coffee, through cream."

One might not want to be quite so stingy with the whiskey, but otherwise the recipe holds true.

IRISH COFFEE

4 oz strong black coffee
1 ½ oz Irish whiskey
2-3 lumps sugar, to taste
Heavy cream

Start with well-chilled heavy cream. Whisk the cream lightly so it is thick but can still be poured. Do not add sugar to the cream.

Heat a glass goblet by rinsing it with hot water. Fill it three-quarters of the way with coffee, whiskey, and sugar, and stir.

Next, touch the surface of the coffee with a spoon turned bowl-down. Pour the cream over the back of the spoon, floating it on top of the coffee. If the cream floats easily, you probably whipped it up a little too stiffly, as getting the cream to float should be a challenge. Don't mix the cream into the coffee. Instead, as old Clementine advised, "sip and the whiskey laces through coffee, through cream."

Though Irish Coffee can be ordered by men without embarrassment, it is no surprise that its first champion in America was a distaff columnist. That simply proves that the feminine influence over the drinks menu is neither new, nor necessarily unfortunate. "It was indubitably the inquiring, adventuring quality of the female mind and the roaming and ravenous interest of the feminine palate that brought the cocktail out of its swaddling clothes into this present vast wardrobe of drink," wrote Crosby Gaige in his *Cocktail Guide and Ladies' Companion*. "Had the cocktail been left to muddling males it would probably have achieved its alpha and omega with the Dry Martini, the Old Fashioned, the Manhattan, and the Daiquiri."

Indeed, the feminine palate is capable of far more than today's rather more egregious sort of "girly drink" gives it credit for. Annabel Meikle leads tasting panels for the Scotch Malt Whisky Society in Edinburgh. Though she admits that women "generally have a slightly sweeter tooth," she finds that once they give Scotch a chance they "have a more discerning palate, which makes them better equipped to pick up more subtle nuances of flavor." They're also more perceptive of the whiskies' other qualities. "Women look at, and care more about, the color of the dram," Meikle says. Asked to describe the color of a given whisky, men tend to give "rubbish descriptors," she says, "like *whisky-colored*." By contrast, women will make fine color distinctions, and "generally use hair color terms, like blonde and auburn."

Francois, a bartender at the ladies-only watering hole at New York's Café des Beaux Arts, would have agreed: "Women are the only people who understand the artistry of mixed drinks. Men pretend to, and use a great deal of language explaining how a mint julep should be made, or how much gin should be used in this or that kind of cocktail, but they are all bluffers," he said. "But the women are different. The artistic sense that is inherent in all of them extends to drinks as well as to everything else."

We may finally be witnessing the last gasps of the Cosmo and its progeny—the jewel-toned "candy-tinis" that have given women's cocktails such a bad name of late. More and more bars are anchoring their drinks lists with classic cocktails, the best of which—whether a Manhattan, a Negroni, or an Old-Fashioned—are balanced enough to bridge the gender divide. But there's always room for new cocktails, and the challenge isn't just one for the bartenders. Women who have indulged their sweet tooth at the bar can make an effort to join their more sophisticated sisters who have learned to appreciate cocktails that actually taste of alcohol; likewise, men who have sought safety in the same old same-old can take a chance on the new—giving mixologists more reason to take masculine tastes into account.

With any luck, men and women will find it easier to get together over a drink—the same drink, that is.

7

COCKTAILS AND COMBAT

BY THE LAST DAYS OF THE CIVIL WAR, THE FORAGING ARMIES HAD drunk the countryside dry. And it was a shortage that nearly prolonged the fighting.

Robert E. Lee may have surrendered to Ulysses Grant on April 9, 1865, but in the weeks to come, the war wasn't quite over. Rebel armies were still in the field, and Confederate President Jefferson Davis was on the loose, still giving orders. Hoping to end the war for good, and to decommission the Southern soldiers in such as way that they didn't disperse into troublesome guerilla forces, Union Gen. William Tecumseh Sherman met with Confederate Gen. Joseph Johnston and the South's Secretary of War, John Breckinridge, at a North Carolina farm. The effort almost foundered then and there, all for the want of a glass of whiskey.

"You know how fond of his liquor Breckinridge was," Johnston would recount years later. Confederate stores of drink had long been exhausted. "For several days, Breckinridge had found it difficult, if not impossible, to procure liquor," Johnston said. "He showed the effect of his enforced abstinence. He was rather dull and heavy that morning."

That is, until Sherman showed up. The Union general arrived with a well-provisioned saddlebag: "Gentlemen," Sherman declared, "it occurred to me that perhaps you were not overstocked with liquor, and I procured some medical stores on my way over. Will you join me before we begin work?'"

It was a good start. Breckinridge "poured a tremendous drink, which he swallowed with great satisfaction." He perked up immediately—and a perky Breckinridge was an impressive sight. Vice President of the United States in James Buchanan's administration, Breckinridge had been one of the smoothest and sharpest lawyers in the country. Fortified, "Breckinridge never shone more brilliantly than he did in the discussions which followed," Johnston said. "He seemed to have at his tongue's end every rule and maxim of international and constitutional law."

Breckinridge was on such a roll that Sherman finally pushed back his chair and blurted: "See here, gentlemen, who is doing this surrendering anyhow?" Flummoxed, Sherman went back to the saddlebag and retrieved the bottle of whiskey. What followed nearly extended the war by months.

Sherman, "preoccupied, perhaps unconscious of his action," proceeded to pour himself—and only himself—a drink. He put the bottle away in the saddlebag and, lost in thought, "sipped his grog." Breckinridge watched in disbelief. According to Johnston, his "face changed successively to uncertainty, disgust, and deep depression."

When Sherman came out of his reverie, he sat down and promptly wrote out a simple, comprehensive peace settlement, the terms of which were far more generous than Johnston or Breckinridge could possibly have hoped for—generous enough that they would get Sherman into trouble with the White House. Breckinridge should have been jumping for joy. Instead, he was bitter and glum.

"General Johnston," Breckinridge said as the two left the meeting, "General Sherman is a hog. Yes, sir, a *hog.* Did you see him take that drink by himself?" he sputtered. "No Kentucky gentleman would ever have taken away that bottle."

The notion that you need a nightcap when putting a war to bed is hardly new. As far as the ancient Greeks were concerned: no drinks, no peace. Indeed, the plural of the Greek word for "libation," *spondai*, is the word for "treaty."

The etymology might seem simple enough—sign a treaty and everyone parties! But the word's origin was more serious than that. The ancient Greeks concluded their treaties with the swearing of oaths consecrated by the pouring of wine. That's how the word for libation came to mean not only treaty, but also any promise. Via Latin, the root has given us such promise-related English words as "respond," which is why one could say, with a certain tortured literalness, that to be "despondent" is to be without a drink.

Soldiers in the field have traditionally not been despondent in that sense—Nelson's navy had its grog, and the hoplites had their wine ration. Even if liquor wasn't part of the soldier's pay package, some determined scrounging would usually turn up something drinkable. As military historian John Keegan writes, "Drinking alcohol before battle is an almost universal practice where wine or spirits are available."

During the Civil War, New York's Fighting 69th was part of what was called the Irish Brigade, led by General Thomas Francis Meagher. When he ran out of fizzy water to mix with his Irish whiskey, Meagher cut his dram with some Champagne conveniently found on a nearby Virginia plantation. One part Irish whiskey to two parts bubbly is still the official regimental drink.

The blue and grey grunts were drinking something a little less fancy—Soldiers' Camping Punch, a recipe for which can be found in Harry Johnson's *New and Improved Illustrated Bartenders' Manual*, published in 1882. You start with four pounds of sugar, four bottles of brandy and two bottles of rum. Light it on fire, and stir it up to dissolve the sugar in the burning spirits. Douse it with "a large kettle of strong black coffee," Johnson writes, and "you will have a good hot punch for soldiers on guard."

Though the modern Army might have a rather different conception of what soldiers on guard should be drinking, the 19th-century Soldiers' Camping Punch warrants making today if you have to soldier out to a football game or some other chilly spot. If you don't have to serve a regiment, try making a small batch with 4 ounces brandy, 2 ounces rum, 4 tablespoons sugar, and 16 to 20 ounces of coffee (to taste). It works best if you put the liquor and the sugar in a wide saucepan and heat it up a bit. Unless you are using dangerously combustible over-proof rum (warning: please refrain from burning your house down), you need to warm the spirits to get them to ignite.

In *Band of Brothers*, Stephen Ambrose writes that for the Allies invading Europe in 1944, "There was just too much booze around." Soldiers fighting their way across France, Belgium, and Italy found that every liberated village "was full of wine, cognac, brandy, and other fine liquor, of a quality and in a quantity quite unknown to the average enlisted man."

The men island-hopping their way across the Pacific ran across no such riches. According to N. E. Beveridge's 1968 book *Cups of Valor*, U.S. Marines managed to come up with an improvised version of what today would be called a stiff Vodka Saketini: They mixed captured Japanese aviation fuel (which was straight ethanol) and rice wine. And there was always "jungle juice," the catchall name for anything alcoholic concocted in the field. Army Sergeant Lyle Hougan described one way of making jungle juice: "the easiest way was to find a green coconut," he told Wisconsin Public Television a couple of years ago. Drill a hole, "then you put in some raisins and sugar and you stuffed a cork in it, set it out in the open. When the cork blew out, she was done."

Whatever the drink, the dangers and deprivations of war have made soldiers appreciate their libations all the more. As Sidney Rogerson—an English company commander who fought at the Battle of the Somme, where on July 1, 1916, twenty thousand British soldiers died in one day— put it, "To enjoy luxury, it is necessary to live hard." In his book about life at the front, *Twelve Days*, Rogerson recalled that in the field, "a tot of rum or whisky and water in a tin mug, taste[d] more like divine nectar than the best Champagne drunk out of the finest cut-glass today."

At the officers' clubs—some way back from the trenches—they *were* drinking Champagne, and mixing it with, of all things, gin. Named after a 75-millimeter artillery piece used in the Great War, the "French 75" cocktail is not the most obvious of drinks. It's gin, lemon juice, and sugar over ice, topped up with Champagne, and it's surprisingly good. The drink was still going strong come the next World War: French 75s are ordered up by a German officer in *Casablanca* not long before Rick's Café Americain is shut down upon the shocking discovery that there is gambling going on there.

FRENCH 75

1½ oz gin
1 oz fresh lemon juice
2 teaspoons sugar
Champagne

Mix gin, lemon juice, and sugar over ice in a tall glass. Top up with Champagne. Garnish with cherry and lemon peel.

On the home front during WWII, civilians did their best to make their drinking part of the war effort by ordering up Victory Cocktails. Of the various Victory drinks made across the country during the war, two common recipes survive. A Victory Highball is made with equal parts of pastis (such as Pernod or Ricard) and grenadine, on the rocks, topped with soda water. I can't say I like it one bit. However, the Victory Cocktail—equal parts sweet and dry vermouth plus a third as much each of orange juice, lemon juice, and grenadine—is refreshing and easy to drink (and nowadays would make a great brunch cocktail).

VICTORY COCKTAIL

¾ oz sweet vermouth
¾ oz dry vermouth
¼ oz orange juice
¼ oz lemon juice
¼ oz grenadine

Shake over ice and strain into a Martini glass.

You might notice that the Victory Cocktail used no hard liquor, which came to be in shortish supply stateside. Like other industries, distillers had been converted to war work. Some cranked out industrial alcohol for synthetic rubber. Others, such as the "Virginia Gentleman" stills, were put to use making torpedo fuel. This gave rise to a cocktail peculiar to submariners and PT boat crews, who, once they realized that the fuel powering torpedoes was straight alcohol, started tapping them. When the Navy brass learned that sailors were draining the fish to get at the "torpedo juice," they had a noxious red chemical added to the fuel to discourage the practice. Not to be denied, the men found that a loaf of bread, with the heels cut off, made an admirable filter. In one end of the bread, they poured the red torpedo juice; out the other end came a marginally less noxious tipple they named with the same wink and nod that tramps applied to their Sterno: "Pink Lady."

This just may solve the problem of how to rescue the real Pink Lady from its gender-limiting name. Drop the egg white from the Pink Lady and you get a fine gin and applejack sour that we can name, with a nod at the submariners' cocktail of convenience, Torpedo Juice. Such a drink even has the virtue of sharing a family resemblance to an old cocktail called the Torpedo, which was made of applejack, cognac, and a dash of gin. Shake it well and strain—though not through a loaf of bread—into a cocktail glass.

TORPEDO JUICE

1½ oz gin
¾ oz applejack (apple brandy)
½ oz fresh lemon juice
¼ to ½ oz grenadine (to taste)

Shake with ice and strain into a stemmed cocktail glass.

Unlike WWII, the wars in Afghanistan and Iraq have yet to produce any drinks, in no small part because American soldiers serving in the Middle East are prohibited from drinking at all. The Pentagon's "general order #1" sets out a long list of verbotens; among them is alcohol, which is banned in deference to Muslim sensibilities.

Given their long, dangerous, and dry stints in the desert, today's returning veterans deserve to be fêted when they get home. Such parties call for a good drink—but what? I asked Dale DeGroff to create a new cocktail in their honor. DeGroff found a 19th-century recipe named after the hero of the War of 1812, "General Harrison's Egg Nog." That drink has hard cider at its core, together with egg and sugar. DeGroff updated Old Tippecanoe by mixing 1 ounce of bourbon with 3 ounces of fresh apple cider, 2 teaspoons sugar, and one raw egg. Shake it over ice until it's good and frothy, and you have a cocktail we've christened the "General Order #1." *Salut*, with a salute.

GENERAL ORDER #1

1 oz bourbon
3 oz fresh apple cider
2 teaspoons sugar
1 fresh egg

Shake with ice and strain into a double Old-Fashioned glass.

8

HERE'S HOW! (AND WHERE)

MY FAVORITE BAR, BLAIR'S BLUE ROOM, CAN BE FOUND ON THE ground floor of a downtown hotel built in the 1920s after an Italianate fashion. What with Prohibition, the space was originally a lounge for tea in the afternoons, and coffee and cigars in the evenings (though if you were a friend of the hotel, your coffee wasn't just coffee). As the name would suggest, upon its conversion into a bar in the 1930s, Blair's was done up all in blue—indigo carpets, azure walls, and a circular banquette of cerulean leather in the middle of the room. The only contrasting notes are the deep mahogany of the long bar and the crisp white of the table linens. Tucked as it is into the corner of the building facing a busy intersection, Blair's Blue Room is not the sort of place one goes for a tryst: tall, arched, and mullioned windows reach from the floor to near the ceiling, and at night, you feel like the bar is part of the glittering life of the city.

There are no TV screens in the bar, and no sound system either.

Free from speakers in the ceiling delivering canned crooners, you can actually have an undistracted conversion with friends there. This isn't to say that there is no music at Blair's Blue Room. Weeknights, there is a jazz pianist named Jimmy who's got enough solid stride in his left hand to keep things swinging even when playing solo. On weekend nights, he's joined by bass and guitar.

Things jump, but they aren't loud: The piano is unamplified, the bass player thumps away without pickup or amp, and even the guitarist plays acoustically. Remarkably, the band doesn't mind if people talk, laugh, or otherwise enjoy themselves. The guys realize that they're there to entertain. Jimmy is happy to take requests, but he has a deft way with the customer who asks to hear something from Barry Manilow or Andrew Lloyd Webber—they never quite know how it was they were persuaded to be happy with Rodgers and Hart instead.

The Blue Room's bartenders actually know their drinks. They can clearly recall the difference between a Rob Roy (two parts Scotch to one part sweet vermouth) and a Thistle cocktail (equal parts Scotch and sweet vermouth), and they can deliver them, reliably distinct from each other, time and again. Their trick for making precision drinks is the simplest and most obvious one—measuring.

Next time you're out at a bar, take note of whether the bartenders measure properly or just pour away. Most eyeball the liquor as it goes straight into the shaker. I'll admit the latter looks more professional— like a chef who knows his ingredients so well that he can grab and toss a smidge of this and a pinch of that. It looks more generous too: Measuring each ingredient can be misperceived as being stingy with the cheer. But meting out the spirits in exact amounts makes for better drinks.

As New Orleans bartender Chris McMillian once told me, "Mixing drinks is more like baking than cooking; having the exact proportions is the difference between success and failure." It's a point on which "Trader" Vic Bergeron was adamant: "My best advice is to make every drink as though it were to be the best you've ever made," he wrote in his 1947 *Bartenders Guide*, "and you can't do this if you don't measure."

ROB ROY

2 oz Scotch whisky
1 oz sweet vermouth
2 dashes Angostura bitters

Shake with ice and strain into a cocktail glass.
Garnish with lemon peel.

THISTLE

1½ oz Scotch whisky
1½ oz sweet vermouth
2 dashes Angostura bitters

Shake with ice and strain into a cocktail glass.
Garnish with lemon peel.

I don't know where Blair's Blue Room keeps all its glasses, which come in an inexhaustible variety of sizes and shapes, each suited to a particular drink. Ask for a fizz or a sour, and it is served in a proper Delmonico glass, not unlike a highball glass but a little bigger and also slightly wider at the top than the bottom. Bigger still is the bar's Collins glass, and they also have the tall, narrow cousin used for

Zombies. There are silver cups for juleps and I've even seen them dig out a copper mug for a Moscow Mule.

The one glass the Blue Room doesn't have is what is now universally known as a Martini glass—the stemmed glass with the conical bowl. Ask for a Martini at Blair's Blue Room, and it comes in the bar's standard cocktail glass, which instead of being V-shaped is curved like an old Champagne saucer, though with a slight flair at the lip. I like not only their glasses, but also that when you ask for a Martini, none of the waiters or bartenders would think to ask, "Vodka, or gin?" It's not that they are opposed to making Vodkatinis. It's just that they realize a Martini is a drink of gin and vermouth.

To quote George Orwell, "Now is the time to reveal something which the discerning and disillusioned reader will probably have guessed already. There is no such place" as Blair's Blue Room.

Actually, when Orwell made his declaration, in a 1946 article for London's *Evening Standard* newspaper, he was writing not of the Blue Room, but about "the Moon under Water." It was his idealized Platonic form of a pub, a fictional Victorian holdout that was free from plastic paneling, radios, and bottled beer. Orwell listed "ten qualities that the perfect pub should have," and lamented that at best he had been able to find a drinking spot that possessed eight of those ten virtues. (London, by the way, now has a chain of joints that have adopted the name "the Moon under Water," but are otherwise without resemblance to Orwell's ideal.)

Sadly, I've never found a bar that has even half of the virtues of Blair's Blue Room. Yes, I know where to find a beautiful hotel bar with big windows that look out on an entertainingly crowded street; I know of exacting bartenders who measure every drink they mix. But there is hardly a drinking room in the country that has the courage to go without the dull laugh-track aesthetic of canned music. Rarer still is the spot that has the right glass for the right drink. But if you know of a bar that comes close, as Orwell said, "I should be glad to hear of it."

Short of the perfect bar, I prefer to find a place with personality, especially if that character is an expression of something unique and uncontrived about the bar's setting. I found that rare organic charm in the little town of Chimayó, which lies in the New Mexico desert.

One bright midday, a week before Easter, I was winding along Route 503 in the high-desert badlands between Santa Fe and Taos. On the crest of a sun-blanched hill littered with scrub pines and sagebrush, I passed a man walking on the narrow gravel shoulder. The road dropped abruptly into a shallow canyon of strawberry-blonde rock, where I saw others ambling along. Over every rise, I found more people walking, some solitary, some families with children, some in large clusters that crowded into the roadway. Many carried small crucifixes; others bore life-size crosses over their shoulders, the ends of the heavy timbers dragging behind them.

These were pilgrims on their way to Chimayó, where there is a small mission church that is sought out for miraculous cures. Even on a glaring spring day, the heavy adobe walls of the Santuario de Chimayó keep the sanctuary cool and dark; the carved gilt panels behind the altar glimmer with candlelight. Thousands trek across New Mexico to the Santuario each year during Holy Week on a quest for healing, be it physical or spiritual.

I was on a pilgrimage of an admittedly less exalted sort—a trip to the birthplace of my favorite tequila drink, the Chimayó cocktail. Just down the road from the Santuario is the Rancho de Chimayó, a restaurant opened in 1965 by Arturo Jaramillo and his wife, Florence (they later divorced). They converted the old family hacienda, built by Arturo's grandfather, Hermenegildo Martinez y Jaramillo in 1890, into a restaurant—a leap of faith that helped convert New Mexico into a culinary destination.

Outside, the Rancho de Chimayó is draped with deep-red strings of chilies, or *ristras*. Inside is a warren of dining rooms, the walls populated by Jaramillo ancestors with the solemn expressions standard to 19th-century photography. Through to the left is a bright sun-porch of a bar, with a soot-streaked shepherd's fireplace and '40s-chic rattan chairs. That's where I sat down with Florence Jaramillo to learn how the restaurant came by its signature drink, a cocktail made with tequila, apple cider, lemon juice, and crème de cassis.

But first, to appreciate the Chimayó cocktail, we need to recognize that tequila is tricky. Like Scotch whisky, tequila has too much personality to be a versatile cocktail base. For all its quirks, or perhaps because of them, the spirit is perfect in a Margarita, which is just about the only way most Americans drink tequila.

To get a sense of the tyranny of the Margarita (a benign dictatorship, I'll admit), just bop around Santa Fe's restaurants and bars. They have extensive drinks lists, but most of those cocktails are permutations of the Margarita. In fact, most aren't even variations on the Margarita recipe so much as combinations of different brands of the spirits—tequila and orange liqueur—used in the drink. Menus might offer a Margarita with El Tesoro *Reposado* tequila and Cointreau, or one made with Herradura Silver tequila and Grand Marnier. Or how about Cuervo Gold with Bols triple sec or Patron *Añejo* tequila with Gran Gala liqueur? Play this game with dozens of tequilas and you get the selection at Maria's New Mexican Kitchen, which serves over 100 brand-specific Margaritas.

Perhaps the reason Arturo Jaramillo was able to break free of the Margarita imperative at the Rancho de Chimayó is that he didn't start out with the notion of concocting a tequila cocktail. The Chimayó valley has long been rich with apple trees, and Arturo was looking for new ways to use the local superabundance of cider. Florence Jaramillo says that her then-husband spent several nights after-hours experimenting behind the bar before they came up with what would become the restaurant's signature drink, and laughs that it wasn't exactly the hardest work they ever did at the restaurant. The fresh apple cider is still the key to the cocktail—it really needs to be unfiltered, the tawny opaque stuff that comes right off the apple press. The touch of cassis— a thick liqueur made in France from blackcurrants—gives the drink a pleasant, pale purplish hue and the sweetness needed to balance the tart lemon juice.

CHIMAYÓ COCKTAIL

COURTESY OF THE RANCHO DE CHIMAYÓ.

1 1/2 oz tequila
1 oz unfiltered apple cider
1/4 oz fresh lemon juice
1/4 oz crème de cassis

Stir in a glass with ice. Garnish with a slice of unpeeled apple.

At its best, travel can introduce us to new drinks as well as new places, and a visit to Chimayó delivers on both counts. But the venue where most of us could stand the best chance of improving the cocktails we consume is in our own homes. It may be hard to find a bar willing to put the effort into making drinks the right way, but there's no reason not to outshine the pros at home. First, you must overcome the attitude that catch-as-catch-can suffices when mixing drinks.

Restaurants have long looked at their bars not as an extension of their kitchens and cuisines, but rather as an easy profit center. Take the ubiquitous Margarita. In most places, it is made with sweet-and-sour mix rather than fresh lime juice. Sweet-and-sour is a dirt-cheap corn syrup and pseudo-citrus base that allows the bartender to knock out a drink in the time it takes to fill a glass—no squeezing of limes, and no measuring out the right amount of simple syrup to balance the acidic juice. Just pour the sour mix, toss in a shot of tequila and a splash of triple sec, and you're done. It's the equivalent of making mashed potatoes from freeze-dried potato flakes, and yet most customers never notice the con. No wonder the bar is where many restaurants make all their money.

Without a course or two at the Culinary Institute of America, it might be hard to learn how to make a meal at home of the quality the average urbanite has come to expect from an upscale restaurant. By contrast, it's relatively easy to learn to mix drinks that match or surpass the offerings of many pricey bars. All one needs are good liquor, fresh ingredients, and a few basic tools—among them, a decent cocktail shaker. It doesn't hurt if that shaker has some style.

With a dinner party at his house fast approaching, Sinclair Lewis's protagonist George Babbitt "moved majestically down to mix the cocktails" in the pantry. Babbitt—whose name serves as the title of Lewis's 1922 novel of middle-American life—"poured with a noble dignity." Unfortunately, Babbitt isn't quite the suave mixologist he thinks himself to be, as he is found "pouring from an ancient gravy-boat into a handleless pitcher."

Why the gravy boat? Ever the prototypical phony, Babbitt "did not possess a cocktail-shaker. A shaker was proof of dissipation, the symbol of a Drinker, and Babbitt disliked being known as a Drinker even more than he liked a Drink." Thus all the skulking about in the basement pantry—not that it dulled Babbitt's enthusiasm for his concoction: "He tasted the sacred essence. 'Now, by golly, if that isn't pretty near one fine old cocktail! Kind of a Bronx, and yet like a Manhattan. Ummmmmm!'"

MANHATTAN

2 oz rye whiskey
1 oz sweet vermouth
A dash or two of Angostura bitters

*Shake—in a cocktail shaker, please—with ice,
and strain into a Martini glass. Garnish with a cherry.*

The same year that *Babbitt* hit the shelves, F. Scott Fitzgerald published *The Beautiful and Damned*, whose protagonist, the upper-crusty Anthony Patch, doesn't mind quite as much as Babbitt about being known as a Drinker. When Patch gets married, a friend gives the happy couple "an elaborate 'drinking set,' which included silver goblets, cocktail shaker, and bottle-openers." Fitzgerald allowed that this was a slightly less conventional "extortion" than the silver Tiffany tea set the Patches also received.

By the 1930s, cocktail sets had become among the most conventional of wedding presents. No doubt many were put to good use, but plenty went the way of other wedding presents: up on the shelf to be used for extra-special entertaining—which is to say, never. That's one reason why it is easy to find great shakers and cocktail glasses from the mid-20th century. On any given day, eBay has hundreds of vintage cocktail shakers on offer. There are utilitarian shakers in stainless steel, arch chrome-plated art-deco icons, glass shakers in cobalt or ruby, elegant sterling silver sets, and very occasionally something from Russel Wright.

In Mary McCarthy's novel, *The Group*, newlywed "Kay's first wedding present, which she had picked out herself, was a Russel Wright cocktail shaker." Made out of spun aluminum, the shaker came with "a tray and twelve little round cups to match—light as a feather and nontarnishable, of course." When Kay throws a cocktail party, she serves up Clover Club cocktails in those little round aluminum cups.

The novel is autobiographical, and McCarthy had her own Russel Wright cocktail set. Leftist politics in New York in the '30s flowed along a river of cocktails, and McCarthy later wrote that "the literary rackets—The Hollywood racket, the New York cocktail-party racket, and the Stalinist racket" were "practically indistinguishable." It seems that all the most fashionable fellow travelers were pouring from Russel Wright cocktail shakers.

I can see why the Wright stuff would appeal to the striving literary bohemian set. The lines and shapes reflected the machine-age craze for industrial design. More important to the socially conscious was that it was made of simple honest materials: spun aluminum, cork, and walnut. Most Deco bar sets are dressed up in chromium—a little too flashy for serious-minded contributors to *Partisan Review*.

Wright designed more than one cocktail shaker. His 1932 version looked like a howitzer shell and has been exhibited as the Metropolitan Museum of Art. And then there is Wright's "Cocktail Hour Set," the one with the little round cups that McCarthy remembered. The shaker is a marvel of counter-programming. When every other designer was making tall slender shakers called "skyscrapers," Wright fashioned a gourd-shaped mixer, a slightly smushed sphere topped with a thick pipe of a neck for holding and pouring. The neck is wrapped in cork for a good grip and to keep one's hand from freezing. When McCarthy bought her set in the thirties, she would have paid about seven dollars. Today, a Russel Wright shaker and tray with a dozen cups can run toward $10,000.

CLOVER CLUB

1 ½ oz gin
1 oz fresh lemon juice
½ oz grenadine
½ teaspoon sugar
1 egg white (fresh or pasteurized)

Shake vigorously with ice—drinks with egg white need extra elbow grease—and strain into little round aluminum Russel Wright cocktail cups, if you can afford them.

Also worth acquiring is the cocktail set considered to be the high-point of bar design, the "Manhattan" cocktail shaker, tray, and cups designed by Norman Bel Geddes for Revere Copper & Brass. It's hard to say what the prolific Bel Geddes was most famous for—the sets he designed for Broadway, his streamlined machines, or the Futurama exhibit he constructed at the New York World Fair in 1939. (Today, more people are probably familiar with his daughter, the actress Barbara Bel Geddes, who played Jimmy Stewart's long-suffering gal pal in *Vertigo*, and later, *Dallas* matriarch Miss Ellie.) But his "Manhattan," the quintessential "skyscraper" shaker, is one of his most enduring designs. A tall cylinder in gleaming chrome-plated brass, accented by eight subtle vertical lines, the Manhattan was haut deco. It is still remarkably modern-looking, particularly compared to, say, Bel Geddes's Buck Rogers-style designs for automobiles.

This isn't to say there wasn't plenty of Buck Rogers-style design in 1930s barware. Perhaps the rarest tchotchke of the era is the "Opco Ice Gun," an enameled steel ray-gun that shoots a violent spray of cracked ice.

My personal preference for actually mixing drinks—as opposed to the museum pieces—is for the glass skyscraper shakers that were introduced in the 1930s and soldiered on through the 1950s. In part, I admire the basic shape of the classic glass "tallboy" shakers—tall, but not self-consciously skinny, and topped with a flattened chrome dome with an offset pouring spout. I particularly like the colored "spun glass" tallboys made for decades by the Imperial Glass Co. of Bellaire, Ohio. These are sociable shakers, big enough to hold 48 ounces: A host with a tallboy shaker can make a round of drinks in one go and not miss out on the party. Whether you choose a modest glass shaker or a towering Bel Geddes masterpiece, the cocktails are guaranteed to taste better than anything poured out of an ancient gravy boat.

Although the shaker is the backbone of the bar, there will be drinks that call for a slushy consistency that is impossible to achieve without a proper bar blender. But whereas shaken and stirred beverages have been around forever, the blended drink is a relatively new institution. One could argue that without a Jazz-Age bandleader named Fred Waring, Daiquiris would all be straight up and Margaritas would all be on the rocks.

I have to admit that I've always been a bit ambivalent about the bar blender. When I was a teen, I went to hear trombonist Bill Watrous at a Phoenix jazz club called the Boojum Tree. Toward the end of the set, Watrous played a tender ballad that finished with a soaring cadenza. It was during the cadenza that someone must have ordered a Piña Colada, because as the trombonist reached the end of the song, his last delicate high note was obliterated by the screech and whir of a blender behind the bar. Watrous dropped his head in disgust and walked off the stage.

The irony is that the blender—that bane of jazz musicians—was brought to market by Waring, whose band, the Pennsylvanians, was one of the most successful "sweet" orchestras of the swing era. (And with whom my grandfather's brother, Ellsworth Felten, just happened to play trombone.) Before the bar blender, nightclubs weren't con-cert-hall quiet, but at least the muted rattling of a shaker has a rhyth-mic quality. The bar blender doesn't do swing time.

The Waring Blendor (the trademarked name is spelled that way) soon became notorious among musicians for its untimely keening. Composer Matt Dennis, for one, got fed up with the thing. Dennis wrote a small raft of songs for Frank Sinatra when Young Blue Eyes was still a skinny kid in Tommy Dorsey's band. Among them was the hit "Everything Happens to Me," the lyric a litany of unfortunate occur-rences. When Dennis would sing it himself in later years on the cabaret scene, he added the line "And when I sing a solo, then the Waring Blendor goes…"

Though he put his name on it, Fred Waring didn't invent the Blendor. Before becoming a bandleader, he had been a mechanical engineering major at Penn State and had a reputation as a tinkerer. This reputation is why an inventor named Frederick J. Osius brought a rough prototype backstage one night in 1936. Waring cut a deal with the man and set about improving the device before having it manufactured.

Not a drinker himself, Waring at first tried to promote his appliance as essential to health fanatics. In 1938, while being interviewed on a radio program called *For Men Only*, he said, "I can mix anything at all. I can fix a health drink that has celery, carrots, cashew nuts, spinach, pineapple juice, anything you ..." The interviewer cut him off: "You don't expect anybody but Popeye to drink that now, do you?" No dummy, Waring immediately switched gears and bragged, "In Florida the other day at a party, I made some 420 frozen Daiquiri cocktails in about an hour and a half."

Mass-producing Daiquiris may not seem a particularly formidable feat nowadays, but at the time the Daiquiri was the sort of drink to make bartenders groan. What with the cracking, chipping, shaving, and crushing of ice needed, the drink was sheer drudgery. "Bartenders hated to make it because it was a tough job by hand," Waring said later. "It took 10 or 15 minutes to make one."

As he traveled the country with his orchestra, Waring would do daytime demonstrations at department stores. Along the way, the bandleader perfected his recipes on a captive audience—the members of his orchestra. Singer Ferne Buckner recalled that as long as Waring was puréeing vegetables, everyone in the band was "casing any and all alternative routes between stage and dressing rooms in each new theater in an attempt to avoid the *thing*." When Waring finally started mixing rum into the equation, the musicians' attitude toward the *thing* changed markedly. Soon, Waring was taking Pennsylvanians with him to put on Blendor shows at Macy's and Bloomingdale's.

Waring did his own celebrity wrangling. One day between shows, he whipped up a Strawberry Daiquiri backstage for his friend Rudy Vallee, the megaphone-amplified crooner, and Vallee became Waring's first salesman. With his own Blendor hidden in a monogrammed case, Vallee would go barhopping night after night, ordering Strawberry Daiquiris. If the bar didn't have a Waring Blendor, he'd take his own machine behind the bar and mix up batches for the crowd. If the bartender did have a Blendor, Vallee would play dumb and loudly marvel at the wonder of the thing.

Even without the celebrity street campaign, it didn't take long for mixologists to see the value of Waring's gadget. "Most cold drinks may be mixed, or shaken, by hand. Of course, underground tunnels may be dug by hand," wrote Charles Baker Jr. in 1939's *The Gentleman's Companion: Being an Exotic Drinking Book*. By then, Waring's blender had produced a "new style Daiquiri, which simply cannot be shaped up by hand at all. There is no wrist strong or deft enough to make any mix of liquid and cracked ice turned into frosted sherbet-like consistency."

"We do not even know Mr. Waring," Baker wrote, "but we like his music and his blender."

A decade later, the Waring Blendor was in just about every bar in the country. Next, Waring's marketing focused on putting the machine in homes. Waring Products Corp. blanketed liquor stores with recipe pamphlets for making frozen "Pickups and Cheerups." Tucked in with the instructions for Strawberry Daiquiris are a few recipes that reflected Waring's taste for kitchen-sink concoctions: anyone for Prune Apple Nectar, with its combination of dry sherry and prune juice? I didn't think so.

Even today, though, Waring's basic Frozen Daiquiri recipe is quite serviceable (though you may want to up the lime and sugar quotient to taste). Just remember, if you've got a little music going on the stereo, before you flip the switch on your blender, please wait till the trombone solo is over.

FROZEN DAIQUIRI

(ADAPTED FROM "HERE'S HOW—THE WARING WAY!" CIRCA 1947)

1 ½ tablespoons lime juice
1 tablespoon sugar
2 oz white-label rum
2 cups finely cracked ice

Place in blender. Hit button.
Feel free to double the amount of lime juice and sugar.

Where to put the blender, the shaker, and all one's liquor for that matter? Skulk in the basement pantry like George Babbitt, if you like, or contest for space in the kitchen—space likely already claimed by coffee makers and toaster ovens. How much more civilized to put it all in a bar of one's own, especially if that bar has a history of its own.

Vintage bars can be bought from dealers such as Architectural Antiques Exchange in Philadelphia, which acquires the interiors of decommissioned British pubs and defunct Belgian cafés. Minneapolis's City Salvage goes hunting for homeless Victorian saloons to rescue, especially the grand, ornate bars carved a century ago by the Brunswick Company. If you've got the space, building a bar of your own is one way to ensure that your favorite local haunt doesn't go out of business or, worse yet, turn into a karaoke bar.

The idea of a home bar hasn't always been applauded. Alma Whitaker, in her 1933 book *Bacchus Behave! The Lost Art of Polite Drinking*, declared, "One of the most deplorable customs that won favor during Prohibition, especially in flamboyant Hollywood, was the home bar." Whitaker was a Tinseltown society columnist for the *Los Angeles Times*, and she had seen plenty of outré antics among the glitterati.

"The home bar idea is far worse than any saloon," Whitaker wrote. "One doesn't have to wait to be invited to drink, and one doesn't have to consider paying for one's own drinks, or standing a round to the crowd when one's turn comes." So far, I'm not quite sure what the problem is. But Whitaker sums it up: "It takes a well-bred person to refrain from being lavish at the expense of some one else." In other words, the home bar encouraged the very excess that led to Prohibition.

But I rather suspect that the excesses Whitaker witnessed were a dysfunction of Prohibition itself, and not of the particular venue. Those putting mahogany slabs in their homes today seem less interested in rumbustion than in creating the sort of clubby, civilized atmosphere lacking in most retail drinking establishments. Even so, the home bar will always have a slightly illicit aura. After all, it is perched on a stool at the bar in her own house—with one leg hiked up, just so—that Mrs. Robinson begins to seduce Benjamin Braddock in *The Graduate*.

The home bar may be vaguely illicit, but it is also eminently practical—a designated place for bottles, glasses, and the rest. In his book *On Drink*, Kingsley Amis includes a section on how to outfit a bar at home. For the most part, he focuses on the specific tools needed—bar spoons, lemon squeezers, corkscrews, and "a really very sharp knife." (As for how to use that knife, Amis suggests, "If you want to finish the evening with your usual number of fingers, do any cutting-up, peel-slicing, and the like before you have had more than a couple of drinks, preferably before your first.") But number one on Amis's list of "Bar Kit" essentials is a dedicated refrigerator of one's own.

"Wives and such are constantly filling up any refrigerator they have a claim on, even its ice-compartment, with irrelevant rubbish like food," Amis writes. What might he have had in his bar refrigerator? Among the bottles might be some freshly squeezed cucumber juice, which he would have used to make a proprietary cocktail named after his first novel, *Lucky Jim*. It's a curious, and not unpleasant, twist on the dry Vodka Martini, a drink that would look fine sitting on one's own slab of vintage mahogany.

THE LUCKY JIM

3 oz vodka
¼ oz dry vermouth
½ oz cucumber juice

Stir with ice and strain into a cocktail glass.
Float a slice of unpeeled cucumber on the top.

Once you've got the knack of making good drinks at your house—whether behind an elaborate bar or just at the kitchen counter—it's time to have a cocktail party. But do try to make it a *cocktail* party.

There is an art to throwing any sort of party, but the cocktail party poses the particular challenge of mixing drinks while simultaneously attempting to socialize, which may explain why so many events advertised as cocktail parties these days end up involving little more than wine and cubed cheese.

The cocktail party is something of an American invention. In colonial days, the local tavern was the place where people met, hatched revolutions, and drank with their pals. And so it went until the 1920s, when Prohibition put the corner saloon out of business. Sure, there were speakeasies, but if you didn't want to risk a raid, you drank at home, and if you wanted to enjoy yourself, you did not drink alone. According to Eric Burns's book *The Spirits of America*, folks whose bathtubs were full of improvised gin "invited their friends to visit, and they kept the glasses as full as they could for as long as they could." (Even if Alma Whitaker disapproved.) Since the hooch was usually of dubious drinkability, the hosts mixed it up into cocktails.

For decades, the cocktail was king of the party, but no longer. Come the '60s, classic cocktails went the way of *The Man in the Gray Flannel Suit*. In the past decade, cocktails have enjoyed a welcome resurgence, but that has yet to translate into many cocktail parties worthy of the name.

One big disincentive to serving cocktails at home is the daunting prospect of getting stuck behind the bar all night struggling to figure out what goes in a Sloe Gin Fizz. (Hint: not gin, but sloe gin, a liqueur made from sloe berries steeped in grain alcohol.) But some hosts actually like tending bar. It offers an easy master-of-ceremonies role. When it got to be a quarter to three and he had a lot of people at his place, Frank Sinatra would play barkeep. Safely behind the bar in his

Palm Springs mansion, he would pour his guests booze in highball glasses etched with Frankie slogans like "Ring-a-Ding-Ding" and "Ol' Blue Eyes." (Sinatra would, I trust, give everyone just the right amount of ice.)

You don't have to get stuck behind the bar at your own cocktail party, unless you want to. Think Nick and Nora Charles in the *Thin Man* movies. Anytime a few old hoodlum friends of Nick's showed up at their apartment, the Charleses threw an impromptu cocktail party. There wasn't a bar in sight. Nick mixed the Martinis in the kitchen and then worked them around the room on a big tray.

What to put on the big tray? Settle on three house drinks for the evening—one gin-based, one whiskey-centric, and one rummy—and you won't have to worry about looking up drink recipes in the wee small hours. They should be drinks that can be mixed in bulk ahead of time and stored in the refrigerator. Since some of your guests will like their drinks on the sweet side and others not, balance the offerings from sweet to dry.

Just be sure to test the drinks yourself before inflicting them on unsuspecting guests. An old friend of mine hosts plenty of cocktail parties for politicos, lobbyists, scribblers, and other dubious types in her Washington home. The drinks at her to-dos are usually first rate, but even experienced party-givers sometimes make the mistake of serving something without sufficient R&D: at one of her parties, "I tried some new, blue cocktail last year that ended up tasting like jet fuel." At evening's end, she found near-full glasses of Windex-hued booze all over the house.

9

THE SPIRITS OF CHRISTMAS

"THERE ARE NO MORE CHRISTMAS STORIES TO WRITE," O. HENRY declares at the start of his Christmas story *Compliments of the Season*. O. Henry sets a somewhat cynical Yuletide scene: "Everywhere the spirit of Christmas was diffusing itself," he writes. "The banks were refusing loans, the pawn-brokers had doubled their gang of helpers, people bumped your shins on the streets with red sleds, Thomas and Jeremiah bubbled before you on the bars while you waited on one foot."

Thomas and Jeremiah was a jokingly highfalutin name for Tom and Jerry, a frothy, hot drink that was once every bit a piece of American Christmas iconography as mistletoe and roasting chestnuts. In the 1880s, the *New York Sun* reported that "fashionable barrooms" at Christmastime would place a "mammoth, richly ornamented, and costly punchbowl" midway on the bar. In it would be a "compound of eggs and sugar" that was "vulgarly called 'dope.'" (The better sort of bartender called it the "preparation.") The sugar-and-egg batter would be ladled into a mug along with some rum, or brandy, or both, and a shot of boiling water. On the top went grated nutmeg.

Damon Runyon's 1932 story *Dancing Dan's Christmas* revolved around the drink: "It is the evening before Christmas, and I am in Good Time Charley Bernstein's little speakeasy in West Forty-Seventh Street, wishing Charley a Merry Christmas and having a few hot Tom and Jerrys with him." By then, Tom and Jerry was a dimly remembered anachronism, but Runyon notes that the drink was "once so popular that many people think Christmas is invented only to furnish an excuse for hot Tom and Jerry."

For the small-time gangster called Dancing Dan, the Tom and Jerry is a lifesaver: Toasted on the holiday tipple, he borrows a Santa suit to go on a gifting spree. Rival gangsters waiting to blast him outside Good Time Charley's joint don't recognize Dancing Dan, what with the Kringle get-up. "There is nothing that brings out the true holiday spirit like hot Tom and Jerry," Runyon writes.

Authorship of the drink has long been attributed to Jerry Thomas, a bartender with enough celebrity in New York that, upon his death in 1885, the *New York Times* delivered a eulogy of several hundred words. That obit credits Thomas with having invented Tom and Jerry in 1847—when the mixologist would have been in his teens—and posthumously quotes him at length on his triumph ("Mr. Thomas never wearied of telling the story of its first concoction"). It seems the young Thomas was working in a saloon out in California when a customer asked for an egg beaten with sugar. "How beautiful the egg and sugar would be with brandy in it!" Thomas thought. He promised the man that "If you'll only bear with me for five minutes, I'll fix you up a drink that'll do your heart-strings good," and went to work mixing egg, sugar, brandy, and hot water. "The drink realized my expectations," Thomas had recounted, and so, inverting his first and last names, "I named the drink after myself."

It turns out Thomas wasn't just a self-promoter; he was a fibber. In 1841, the *Bangor Whig* newspaper printed a lugubrious temperance ditty called "Death's Allies." Among the drinks doing the Grim Reaper's work were Toddy, Punch, and Flip—and Tom and Jerry. If the holiday drink was well enough known to make it into an anti-alcohol song, it must have been in circulation quite some time—a decade, at least—that is, from about when Jerry Thomas was born.

The drink almost certainly got its name from a hugely popular English novel, *Life in London*, which was written by Pierce Egan in 1821. The tale follows the rambunctious exploits of "Jerry Hawthorne and his elegant friend Corinthian Tom," two rascal gadabouts who put on airs as they get up to mischief. The book (and later, play) inspired a raft of popular patois in England and the U.S. A certain sort of rakish top hat was called a Tom and Jerry. Roguish waistcoats got the moniker, too. But mostly, Tom and Jerry was used to describe things drinks-related.

Indiana University slang scholar Michael Adams points out that a couple of Tom and Jerrys (rowdies) could go to a Tom and Jerry shop (a dive bar), where they would drink too many Tom and Jerrys "and then terrorize the city with their tom and jerryism." So ingrained in the American language was the phrase that President Benjamin Harrison couldn't give cabinet positions to both Thomas Palmer and Jeremiah Rusk because, as the *Buffalo*

Courier claimed in 1889, "it would never do to have Tom and Jerry at Cabinet meetings."

Damon Runyon lamented, "Since Tom and Jerry goes out of style in the United States, the holiday spirit is never quite the same," but there is one place where the holiday spirit is indeed the same, and then some: The Brass Rail Bar in Port Huron, Michigan. Helen David converted the family candy store into a bar in 1937 and ran it for near-ly 70 years until her death in 2006. She kept the holiday tradition of Tom and Jerry alive, whipping up the first batch of batter every year a week before Thanksgiving and pouring the last Tom and Jerry of the season each New Year's Eve at midnight.

The Brass Rail is still going strong, and it may be the capital-N nicest bar I've ever been in. The waitresses have all worked there for 30 years or so, and they greet you with a cheery "Hi, hon, what'll you have?" During the holidays, you can get a tan from the glare of Christmas lights that cover every inch of wall not already taken up by pictures of Little League teams and local hockey players. The rococo, carved backbar is nearly obscured by a tremendous Christmas tree. Off to the side stand the three white KitchenAid mixers that constant-ly worry the "dope."

At the Brass Rail, you can get a Tom and Jerry with brandy and rum, or just about any liquor you like; the house favorite is made with Baileys Irish Cream. It comes in an old Christmas coffee mug, froth-ing and bubbling with Christmas spirit, just as it did in O. Henry's day. If you can't make it to Michigan at Christmastime, make your own batch of the "preparation," and prepare to do your part to revive a lost American tradition.

TOM AND JERRY

½ cup batter
1 oz brandy
1 oz rum
hot water

*Ladle batter into a heated mug. Pour in liquor and then fill
with boiling hot water. Top with grated nutmeg. Let cool just enough
to be drinkable, and serve with a spoon for stirring. For an even
sweeter take on the holiday drink, substitute Baileys for the brandy.*

TOM AND JERRY BATTER

*Separate the whites and yolks of 4 eggs. Whip the egg whites,
with a sprinkle of cream of tartar, until they are stiff.
Fold in 3/4 cup powdered sugar and the egg yolks. Mix until the
batter is light and frothy. Makes enough for about 8 drinks.*

Though a decidedly American tradition, Tom and Jerry has English overtones—the drink is hot, rich with eggs, and dusted with nutmeg—but Tom and Jerry never did catch on in the British Isles. I think that's because the Brits' cup of holiday cheer was already well filled with a drink called Bishop, a drink that had its brightest moment in Charles Dickens's *A Christmas Carol*.

"A Merry Christmas, Bob!" says the reformed Scrooge to Bob Cratchit, as he claps him on the back. "A merrier Christmas, Bob, my good fellow, than I have given you for many a year! I'll raise your salary, and endeavor to assist your struggling family, and we will discuss your affairs this very afternoon over a Christmas bowl of smoking bishop, Bob!"

Bishop, a rich, hot winter punch, is hardly the first bowl of liquor to make an appearance in the story. When Scrooge peeks out from his bedclothes to find the Ghost of Christmas Present in all his jolly opulence, the Giant is surrounded by a great feast, with "seething bowls of punch, that made the chamber dim with their delicious steam." When the Ghost of Christmas Past spirits Scrooge off to the Christmas party of his youth—a dance at the Fezziwigs'—a punch called "Negus" is on the sideboard.

For Dickens, Christmas wasn't Christmas without a steaming bowl of punch. When Mr. Pickwick and his pals go to Dingley Dell for the holiday, they are served a "mighty bowl of wassail" so large that the host proclaims, "It will be two hours, good, before you see the bottom of the bowl." The Wassail would have been made by heating ale and sherry with sugar, ginger, nutmeg, cloves, cinnamon and roasted apples. When the Wassail was brought before Pickwick, "the hot apples were hissing and bubbling with a rich look, and a jolly sound, that were perfectly irresistible." What with the company and punch, Mr. Pickwick proclaims, "this is, indeed, comfort."

Comfy and cozy, no doubt, but not quite cozy enough to overcome the fact that hot, spiced beer mixed with baked apples tastes about as good as it sounds. One almost suspects that Wassail was saved for the holidays so that it would be safely off the menu the rest of the year. Bishop, on the other hand, is actually delicious.

Bishop has been around at least from the 1750s, when Samuel Johnson defined it as "a cant word for a mixture of wine, oranges, and sugar." By the turn of the last century, Bishop was already fading from the popular mind in England. Professor George Saintsbury, a prominent literary critic, was one of its last boosters. In 1920, he lamented, "I have found more people not know than know in this ghastly thin-faced time of ours," that Bishop is "simply mulled Port." The sly old Don proclaims, "It is an excellent liquor, and I have found it quite popular with ladies."

To make a bowl of Bishop, start by studding a couple of lemons or oranges with half a dozen cloves each and roast the fruit in an oven until they are browned. Cut the fruit in half and put it in a saucepan with mulling spices and about a half-pint of water. Boil about half the water away before adding a decent bottle of ruby port into the pan; heat it slowly until it steams, but don't let it boil. "Sugar or no sugar at discretion," says Professor Saintsbury, "and with regard to the character of the wine."

In Dickens's London, Bishop would have been made with clove-studded oranges; it was up at Oxford where the taste ran to roasted lemons with port. I much prefer the Oxonian version, as roasting brings out a bitterness in oranges but takes the sour edge off of lemons. Because of that, I find you don't need as much sugar when using lemons.

When the wine has steeped just below a simmer for a good hour in the citrus and spices, it's ready to drink. However, there is one more step that Professor Saintsbury recommends: setting the Bishop on fire. "The flames will be of an imposingly infernal colour, quite different from the light-blue flicker of [burning] spirits." This tradition may be why old Scrooge calls it a "smoking" bowl. However, be warned that port catches fire about as easily as soggy kindling – the alcohol content just isn't high enough for reliable combustion. I say put away the matches and grab the ladle.

As tasty and festive as a nice, smoking Bishop is, hot wine is less suited to American tastes than British ones. Just as we Americans have found a way to make just about anything into a sandwich, we have also found a way to put just about any drink over ice. Bishop is no exception. Jerry Thomas's 1862 *Bartender's Guide* included a "Protestant" Bishop on the rocks. And "Trader Vic" Bergeron's 1947 bar book listed three different iced "Bishop" cocktails, the best of which is called a Bishop's Cooler—the juice of half a lemon and half an orange, a little sugar, 3 ounces of Burgundy wine and half an ounce of rum over cracked ice in a highball glass. And though it's not in Trader Vic's recipe, add a little soda water while you're at it.

BISHOP'S COOLER

½ lemon
½ orange
1 tsp sugar
3 oz Burgundy
½ oz Jamaican rum

Squeeze lemon and orange over cracked ice in a 10-oz. glass; add sugar and stir. Add burgundy and stir; float the rum.

A Bishop's Cooler wouldn't have had the same resonance as punch in Dickens's story. That's because punch—which isn't measured out glass by glass like a drink poured from a bottle—is a communal drink, a generous, open-handed drink. In other words, the host who lays out a bowl of punch is no scrooge. Of all the outward signs of the miser's redemption, the final confirmation of Scrooge's transformation comes when he takes ladle in hand to serve up the Bishop.

CHRISTMAS BOWL OF BISHOP

2 lemons
½ pint water
Whole mulling spices
1 bottle ruby port
¼ cup sugar, more or less, to taste

Stud two lemons with half a dozen cloves each.
Roast the lemons for half an hour, more or less, in a 350-degree oven.
Cut the roasted lemons in half and put them into a saucepan
with half a pint of water and whole mulling spices, such as cinnamon,
allspice, ginger, mace, and star anise. Don't use powdered
spices, which will make the drink sludgy. Boil off a little of the water
before adding the port, and then sugar to taste.
Be sure not to boil the wine, but let it steep just below a simmer
for an hour. If the punch is too strong, add a little more water.
Serve steaming in punch cups or London dock glasses.

On the last page of *A Christmas Carol*, Charles Dickens indulges himself in a little pun at the expense of teetotalers, writing that after Scrooge's night spent with ghosts, "He had no further intercourse with Spirits, but lived upon the Total Abstinence Principle ever afterward."

The Total Abstinence Principle was the enthusiasm of an old Dickens friend, George Cruikshank, an artist who had illustrated *Oliver Twist*. A reformed alcoholic, Cruikshank crusaded for prohibition. In particular, he tried to take up the Hogarthian mantle, inking morality cartoons on the evil of drink: first, *The Bottle*, and then

The Drunkard's Children. He also drew a series of fairy tales, reinter-
preting classic stories so they imparted a dry message (the problem
with the giant atop Jack's beanstalk, you see, was that he was a mean
drunk). Dickens particularly objected to these humorless rewrites,
mocking them as a *Fraud on the Fairies.*

Dickens was well aware of the suffering—and the stints in the poor
house—that followed from alcohol abuse. He bemoaned boozing that
begins "in sorrow, or poverty, or ignorance—the three things in
which, in its awful aspect, it *does* begin." But Dickens defended the
moderate, social enjoyment of drink as a key part of that "season of
hospitality, merriment, and open-heartedness." So come the holidays, let's raise a steaming glass of Bishop to toast Christmas, "that
happy state of companionship, and mutual good-will, which is the
source of such pure and unalloyed delight, and one so incompatible
with the cares and sorrows of the world." Cheers, indeed.

NIGHTCAP

CHARLES DICKENS WASN'T THE ONLY ONE WHO SAW A METAPHOR FOR friendship and life well lived in a bowl of punch. Oliver Wendell Holmes, Sr. (not *Junior*, the jurist, but his father, the physician and popular poet) once penned an ode to a punchbowl that was resonant with the ritual and tradition of civilized drinking.

> This ancient silver bowl of mine—it tells of good old times,
>
> Of joyous days, and jolly nights, and merry Christmas chimes;
>
> They were a free and jovial race, but honest, brave, and true,
>
> That dipped their ladle in the punch when this old bowl was new.

When we dip that ladle, Holmes suggests, we share in a small way in the virtues of those who ladled before us. It's a simple, direct way to connect with that lost world. "I love the memory of the past," writes Holmes, no doubt a sentimental old softie. Contemplating his ancient silver bowl, Holmes's "eyes grow moist and dim/To think of all the vanished joys that danced around its brim." One could say the same of a well-worn shaker and the many forgotten parties it enlivened. Fill that shaker up today, and it holds more than just liquor and ice.

Holmes imagines Miles Standish mixing a bracing draught in the old punchbowl at a moment when the Mayflower seemed lost; he sees an anguished mother sending her son off to fight at Bunker Hill, ladling him a cup of resolve from the same bowl. Cocktails can work that way, too, connecting us with our past, and reviving lost ways of living.

But what ways of living? It's all too easy to romanticize the more flamboyant excesses of creative types whose genius, like a genie, seems to reside in a bottle. But drink didn't make Hemingway clever. Kingsley Amis cranked out a prodigious body of work in spite of his deep thirst, not because of it. Mencken may have argued that Jack London, sober, never would have written anything worth reading, but the truth is, all the sauce did for London was kill him.

Recommending good things to drink is an enterprise fraught with moral peril. Encourage folks to try a cocktail, and there are sure to be some among them some who—like Bill Wilson with that first Bronx cocktail—will like it altogether too much. I come from a family of tee-totalers. One reason my father, a jazz musician, is not a drinker is that he witnessed the toll the bottle took on many of his friends. On my mother's side of the family was a great-grandfather whose taste for whiskey was the stuff of Anti-Saloon League pamphlets. I have his shot glass, which is deceptively toy-like and shaped like a miniature beer mug. Given the pain that tiny cup caused my grandmother and her siblings, it's odd that she kept it; she certainly didn't keep it in sight. But I do: the glass sits on a high shelf of my liquor cabinet, a cautionary talisman.

Walker Percy, in his article on the joys of drinking bourbon neat, worried that he was doing his audience no favor. "An apology to the reader is in order," Percy offered, "for it has just occurred to me that this is the most unedifying and even maleficent piece I ever wrote – if it should encourage potential alcoholics to start knocking back Bourbon neat." But he concluded that it was worth the danger given the anomie-fighting qualities of Kentucky whiskey.

In the right doses, whiskey fights more than fin-de-millennium blues. Doctors don't mind passing on the word that a daily glass or two of wine is entirely salubrious; but the responsible medical establishment has been positively discomfited by the research showing that it is the alcohol—as opposed to some grapey anti-oxidants peculiar to wine—that makes a Pinot-a-day healthful. The AMA is less than eager to start urging patients to knock back a couple of bourbons a day.

I understand their reticence, but I can't say I endorse it. Where would we be if we tried to quash every perilous pleasure? (That is, where, other than Saudi Arabia...) More than a few people have been undone by love, but we don't abjure it. Rather, one of the central storylines in the history of civilization has been the effort to make love livable.

A good drink, though not without risk, can be eminently livable. Alcohol is no doubt a drug, but in moderation it is a very social one. It primes the conversational pump; it nudges the shy from the bonds of their awkwardness; it midwives romance; it concludes treaties. Firewater, like fire, can be awesomely destructive; learning to marshal the power of both is a hallmark of civilized living.

A proper cocktail connects us with each other even more than it connects us with the past. At its best, a good drink is a sort of secular communion, a cup of fellowship. In his book, *Martini, Straight Up*, Classics professor Lowell Edmunds describes the making of Martinis as a shared ritual, and champions what he calls the "communal" Martini. Martini-drinkers are united in their commitment to the classic recipe, a secular "sacramental drink that unites in spirit even those who have never met."

This isn't to say the ritual is solemn; it's anything but. For F.D.R., cocktail time—the Children's Hour, he called it—was the respite from a hard day's war-making.

If the cocktail hour was once widely observed, it is no longer. People drink, no doubt, but few of us structure our day around what Bernard DeVoto breathlessly called *The Hour.* We might catch a drink here or there with friends, or perhaps even a proper pre-prandial cocktail to get in the mood for dinner. But the way we live now may be both too casual and too frantic for the formality of ritual.

At least that takes the pressure off the poor little cocktail, which couldn't but groan under all that weight of Meaning and Importance. Amusement is the cocktail's real line of work, and a noble one at that. Harry Craddock, the legendary barman at London's Savoy Hotel in the 1920s, told his customers that the best way to drink a cocktail is "while it's laughing at you!" Spot on. Just be sure to laugh back.

If there is anything to be serious about in the way of drinks it is this only: that one's drink be delicious. If it can add to our pleasure by having a good story to tell, then all the better. Great drinks are like the tunes from the Great American Songbook: they can withstand the endless permutations that come from individual interpretation. Enjoying those drinks makes one part of a living tradition—a lineage of civilized drinkers.

"Then fill a fair and honest cup, and bear it straight to me," Holmes urges. "The goblet hallows all it holds, whate'er the liquid be." I have to admit that's where Holmes loses me. *Whate'er the liquid be* isn't quite good enough. Why waste an all-hallowing goblet on anything less than a well-made cocktail? That way, there will never be any doubt about the answer when you're asked, "How's your drink?"

INDEX

ACKNOWLEDGMENTS

MANY THANKS TO THE CRACK TEAM OF EDITORS WHO HAVE MADE ROOM for *How's Your Drink?* in the pages of the *Wall Street Journal*, and who have saved me from committing a superabundance of solecisms: Paul Gigot, Dan Henninger, Eric Gibson, Barbara Phillips, Michael Philips, Tom Weber, and Erich Eichman.

Thanks go to my agent, Esther Newberg, and the rest of the good folks at ICM, and also to the publisher and impresario of Agate/Surrey Books, Doug Seibold.

I'm indebted to all the friends who encouraged this folly, including such valued friends and conspirators as Rudy Maxa, Philip Chalk, Steve Munson, and Peter Scott. Thanks also to all my Palisades pals who found themselves put upon to taste eighteen permutations of some long- (and sometimes duly) forgotten cocktail. Among the good sports are the Gregorys, Rosenbergs, Ryans, Scotts, Sneddens, Sulsers, and Summers.

I'm grateful to my abstemious parents, Lester and Barbara, for their love, support, and example. Thanks—and Horse's Necks—go to my children, Priscilla, Greta, and Thaddeus (who will each get a copy of this book upon turning 21). And most of all, thanks to my wife, Jennifer.

ABOUT ERIC FELTEN

ERIC FELTEN WRITES THE CELEBRATED COCKTAIL COLUMN *How's Your Drink?* for the Weekend Edition of the *Wall Street Journal*. In May 2007, he was honored with a James Beard Foundation award for Best Newspaper Writing on Wine, Spirits, or Beer.

A jazz singer, trombonist, and bandleader, Mr. Felten has recorded five CDs. His public television concert special, *The Big Band Sound of WWII*, has been seen on PBS stations nationwide.

He lives in Washington, DC with his wife and three children.